The Seventh Expert
An Interactive Medieval Adventure

by Mark Oakley illustrated by John Mantha

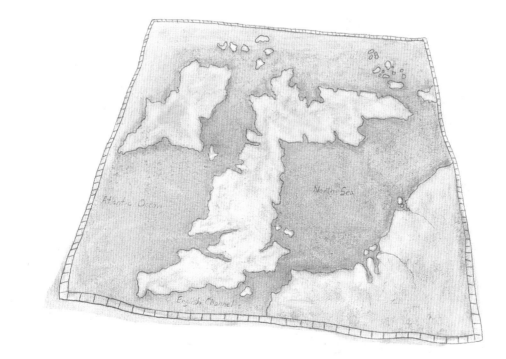

annick press
toronto + new york + vancouver

We acknowledge the support of the Canada Council for the Arts, the Ontario Arts Council, and the Government of Canada through the Book Publishing Industry Development Program (BPIDP) for our publishing activities.

 ONTARIO ARTS COUNCIL
CONSEIL DES ARTS DE L'ONTARIC

All dice ©iStockphoto Inc./Joachim Angeltun; all scrolls ©iStockphoto Inc./Anne Dala.

Cataloging in Publication

Oakley, Mark, 1970-
    The seventh expert : an interactive Medieval adventure /by Mark Oakley ; illustrated by John Mantha.

Includes bibliographical references.
ISBN 978-1-55451-066-5 (bound).—ISBN 978-1-55451-065-8 (pbk.)

    1. Adventure games—Juvenile literature. 2. England—Civilization—1066-1485—Juvenile literature. 3. Civilization, Medieval—Juvenile literature. 4. Middle Ages—Juvenile literature. I. Mantha, John II. Title.

GV1469.62.S48O23 2008   j793.93   C2008-901532-0

Distributed in Canada by:
Firefly Books Ltd.
66 Leek Crescent
Richmond Hill, ON
L4B 1H1

Published in the U.S.A. by:
Annick Press (U.S.) Ltd.
Distributed in the U.S.A. by:
Firefly Books (U.S.) Inc.
P.O. Box 1338
Ellicott Station
Buffalo, NY 14205

Printed in China.

Visit us at: www.annickpress.com

ACKNOWLEDGEMENTS:
The author would like to thank everybody who put up with his months of thinking aloud as he worked through the more puzzling aspects of this project, and for the many inspiring conversations which resulted. Thank you especially to his friends Ian, the history buff, and Richard, the game-and-comic-shop owner. Further special thanks to Bert Hall, Professor at the Institute for the History and Philosophy of Science and Technology, University of Toronto. Thank you also to the game-testers: the students of Robert Teuwen's grade 7 class and Paula Rosa's grade 8 class at Alan Howard Waldorf School in Toronto, as well as Joshua Boughner, Piers Edlund-Field, and Alfredo Paraizo.

SELECTED SOURCES:
Books consulted include: *The Black Death* by Joseph P. Byrne (Greenwood Press, 2004); *The Little Ice Age: How Climate Made History 1300–1850* by Brian M. Fagan (Basic Books, 2000); *Life in a Medieval Village* by Frances and Joseph Gies (Harper & Row, 1990); *Ancient and Medieval Siege Weapons: A Fully Illustrated Guide to Siege Weapons and Tactics* by Konstantin Nossov (The Lyons Press, 2004); and *Agricultural Implements* by Sian E. Rees (Shire Archaeology Publications, 1981).
Websites consulted include: www.britainexpress.com/History/medieval_britain_index.htm, www.cpat.org.uk, medievalhistory.suite101.com/, www.middle-ages.org.uk, the-orb.net/, and www.timeref.com.

Thank you, Ariell, Ian & Zanne, Frank & Myretha, Trent, Richard, Darren, Carson, Tanis, Heather & Jason, and David W.
—M.O.

For my wife, Leanne
—J.M.

Table of Contents

How to Play
The Seventh Expert

This book is not like most others. It is both a story *and* a game.

The story that begins on page 6 is set in medieval England during a time of great upheaval, when the people needed guidance and good fortune to survive the disasters of the age. You are going to help them!

To do this, you will use the **Experts' Catalog**, which starts on page 72. It is a catalog of useful equipment and projects that your people can build or undertake to help them survive and prosper.

Each chapter in the story is one year in the life of your people. At the end of each chapter, you will find a short list of game instructions. To follow them, you will need a six-sided die, a pencil, and paper to keep track of your scores.

Make a score chart with headings for your items and the three scores you'll be tracking:

SCORE CHART

ITEM	EFFORT	SUPPLIES	DEFENSE

Make a separate chart to keep track of your Permanent Items (more about this below):

PERMANENT ITEMS CHART

PERMANENT ITEM	YEARLY BONUS

You can also visit www.annickpress.com to download ready-made charts that you can print and use.

WHAT THE SCORES MEAN

Effort points represent how much energy your people have to spend. Any **Effort** points not used before the end of each chapter will be lost.

Supplies are the material resources such as food, wood, and stones that your people use to build equipment and undertake projects. These points are carried over from one chapter to the next. Beware! If **Supplies** ever fall below zero, you lose the game.

Defense points express how well your people can repel attacks by invaders. **Defense** points are carried over from one chapter to the next.

HOW TO PLAY THE GAME

First read the story that begins each chapter and find out what events befall your people that year. Next, read the instructions page that follows each story. You will be told how many points to place on your score chart. You will then be asked to visit the **Experts' Catalog** to spend your points. Your choices as you deal with the challenges faced in each chapter will cause the scores to go up and down.

THINGS TO KNOW ABOUT THE EXPERTS' CATALOG …

Prerequisite Items: Some items in the **Experts' Catalog** have **Prerequisites**, which are other items you must purchase first. Be sure to select items in the proper order and record them on your score chart, for example:

SCORE CHART

ITEM	EFFORT	SUPPLIES	DEFENSE
YEAR ONE	1,000	100	0
Spinning Whorl	700	350	No change
Cord and Rope	600	No change	No change
Bow and Arrow	400	No change	200

Permanent Items: An item marked with a ➤ is Permanent. You only need to purchase that item *once* and then you will always have it as a Prerequisite. Some Permanent Items will also give you a Yearly Bonus *every chapter* after being purchased. Note any bonuses on your Permanent Item chart, for example:

PERMANENT ITEMS CHART

PERMANENT ITEM	YEARLY BONUS
Spinning Whorl	0
Wooden Farming Tools	0
Small Livestock	+200 Supplies

Don't worry too much about remembering all this right now. You'll quickly figure out how to keep track of things as you play the game.

Got your blank charts ready? Then prepare to begin your medieval adventure! The year is 1362 …

PROLOGUE

The Storm

MARCUS YANKED AT HIS BOOTS, SHOVING HIS FEET INTO THEM. Freezing rain pelted through the open door, filling the house with wind, blowing his black hair like a horse's tail.

"Just leave the boats be, Marcus!" his wife cried. "Only madmen dare be outside tonight in such a storm!"

"No!" he bellowed against the wind. "If the boats are not pulled high enough ashore, this storm will sweep them away!"

His wife stood before him, torn between love and the urgency of the situation. They both knew that losing the little fishing fleet would mean many in the town would starve. Farms had long since failed to produce crops. Summers had grown so cold that shorn sheep would freeze in the fields while grazing on the pathetic greens growing there.

"Quickly, Marcus!" urged one of the fishermen outside the door. "There's no time to lose!"

Marcus was a carpenter. Although he did not know the ocean or storms as well as his companions, he had helped to build many of their boats. And now they desperately needed his help.

"Go ahead, then! I'll catch up with you!" He turned to his wife again. "Don't you worry, my love. Port Haven has seen worse than this." It was a brave lie, and both of them knew it.

As Marcus stepped out into the howling darkness, he was almost blinded by the driving sleet. He could barely make out

Storm Surge

The 13th to the 15th centuries marked a time of violent weather in Europe. A period of global cooling caused huge storms and unpredictable ocean tides. In 1413, the village of Forvie, near Aberdeen, Scotland, was buried under a 30-meter (98-foot) sand dune after a strong storm surge.

the knot of fishermen ahead of him, struggling down to the sea. Even their experienced hands and legs slipped and clung, the familiar stones of the path made alien in the storm. A pair of the men lost their footing and at once the wind battered them from the path. Down they tumbled, vanishing into the sheets of rain and hail. Their cries were drowned out by the roar of an ocean that seemed much too near.

Lightning flashed, exposing the world in a moment of brilliance, and Marcus fell to his knees. "It cannot be!" he gasped.

The little crescent beach of Port Haven, used for generations as its harbor, was gone. It had been swallowed entirely in a violence of churning water. The boats were nowhere to be seen.

"COME BACK!" he cried desperately to the fishermen, but his voice was lost in the wind even as the water surged up the rocks. A mighty wave heaved up as though the ocean itself were standing, towering over the small huddle of fishermen.

A Little Ice Age

Cooler seasons were hard on European farmers. Crops rotted in the muddy earth where they were planted. In 1316–17 in Hindolveston Manor, Norfolk, many farmers were unable to pay land rent to their lords because of crop failures. The 1316 grain crop in Winchester was only 56 percent of normal—the lowest amount between 1271 and 1410.

It seemed to hang for a moment, an impossible mountain of water. Then, with a bone-shaking thunder Marcus would remember forever, it crashed down. When the black waters sucked back, Marcus gasped—not one of the fishermen remained.

IN JANUARY 1362, AN IMMENSE STORM SYSTEM DESCENDED upon Europe. From Denmark to northern England, many thousands of lives were lost. To this day, the Dutch still speak of that time as "The Great Drowning of Men."

Our story begins in that same year in England, where the coast meets the Irish Sea. North of Liverpool there is a region of land separating Scotland and England but belonging to neither country. These Border Marches are struggled over by ruthless lords and outlaws. Just south of the Marches, the community of Port Haven has been destroyed by the great storm. Those who did not escape to high ground will never be seen again. Those who survive cluster on a hillside, lost and confused, in need of leadership …

A Town Lost

The community of Bilsdale, in northeast Yorkshire, was thriving in 1300 but abandoned by 1330 because of famine, disease, and disaster. Such dramas were common throughout England and continental Europe.

You Are a Leader

You are a survivor of the disaster. You are neither a lord nor a king nor a soldier. You are but a simple laborer who grew up in Port Haven and who has earned the respect of your neighbors. Whenever people have disagreed with each other, they have found that your carefully considered words solved their problems and encouraged them to end their quarrels with sincere apologies. Whenever calamity has struck, it has been you who leaped first to help in any way you could. The people of Port Haven have come to respect and trust you. The frightened survivors now turn to you for guidance.

After the storm, you all gather on a hill overlooking the destruction. It is time to discuss what needs to be done. Some people suggest it would be best to travel south to the city of Liverpool. However, others have learned from some tinkers—people who travel from place to place mending tin and pots to earn their living—that Liverpool can provide no refuge. It too has been beset with flooding, disease, and hunger.

After careful thought, you suggest that the time has come to travel inland and there begin building a new community. With Port Haven swept away, the people agree. The decision is made to quit the coast.

The men and women of Port Haven have long been known for their strength of heart and good cheer; these qualities will be important in the coming days. But you also know that you will need honed skills and deep knowledge to survive in a new land. Looking to your people, you seek those with such resources. You are fortunate enough to find six worthy individuals who will help you lead the others.

The Seven

Sir Greggor Knight, Siege Engineer

Five months ago, a ship was destroyed in a mighty gale off the coast of Port Haven. From its wreck, a single amazing survivor was rescued. Powerful and burly, with wisps of gray in his black mustache, Sir Greggor Knight was carried, waterlogged and broken-legged, up from the sea. Nursed back to health by your people, the good-natured giant has developed a deep gratitude for the kindness shown to him. As Sir Greggor now reminds you, he used to be a Siege Engineer for a lord in Liverpool, a center of shipbuilding and war technologies.

Sir Greggor Knight

"Until I washed up on your shores, I was in charge of my lord's catapults and field guns and battering rams—all the equipment needed to make war against the enemy.

"Since I was a boy, I have spent my life learning all the trades needed to keep soldiers alive under the harshest of conditions. I know how to make and mend catapults. I know how to manage teams of horses. And, most important of all, I know how to keep order among the troops. I am yours to command!"

You gaze thoughtfully at the man before you, his stance firm and resolute. "Your skills would be of great value to us," you say. "But why would you want to join with us when you could serve in Liverpool? Your position there was filled with glory and status, while our journey will be hard and may end in misery."

Sir Greggor frowns at this. "In all of the stories I have told you since I first arrived, I have kept from you one shameful detail. The truth is that my lord was a vile man and all his wars were evil things. I am ashamed to say that I gave my skills to serve ill causes, and I no longer wish to be a part of it. When I washed up half dead on your beach, I believe I was being granted a second chance to do something better with my life. And here it is!"

Greggor turns his earnest face toward yours, his eyes bright and sincere. "It would be my deepest honor to be allowed to serve in your quest."

Cutting through your tiredness and the cold of your wet clothes, a beam of warmth fills your heart and body when you hear his words. You grasp the great man's shoulders and say, "Thank you, Sir Greggor. You are most welcome among us!"

Mirriam Wise, Homestead Elder

Mirriam is the oldest woman in Port Haven, short in stature and as gnarled and tough as a knotted tree root. Yet Mirriam remains spry of limb and her eyes shine with a wise compassion that makes her face beautiful. She has always been a beacon of comfort to your people. Indeed, many in Port Haven were born into her experienced hands. Mirriam is trusted by the community for guidance in all matters of house, home, and family.

Now she comes over to you and pats your shoulder reassuringly. She has watched you grow up into a community leader and is especially fond of you. "Never worry, my dearie," she says. "Times such as these are difficult and they cause us to fear, but we shall get through with a spot of common sense and tidy work."

Mirriam Wise

"Mirriam," you reply, "I am glad you are confident. Our people will have great need of that quality in the days to come." You turn to her earnestly. "I must be able to count on you, Mirriam, to advise me with wisdom. Are you prepared for that?"

Her face softens and she sighs. "I have been alive for longer than any here can remember and I know some of the most important things we'll be needing to know. I grew up on a farm before I came to Port Haven. Did you know that? I know how and when to plant, and when and what to pick. I know how to make and how to mend.

"Cooking stews and curing sickness, sowing seeds for tomorrow's bread, and mending anything from bones to breeches—oh, I know it all, and I will keep our people busy with it. So don't fret, my dear. So long as you give me the means and the hands, I shall solve the most trying of your troubles, and make things dry and strong in whatever new home you lead us to. Yes, my dearie"—she nods with assurance—"you can count on me."

You place a hand on Mirriam's shoulder and smile at her, much encouraged to have her among your experts.

Marcus Wainwright, Master Carpenter

Marcus can build nearly anything, from buildings and barrels and boats to ornate furniture. He is wise in all the ways wood can be used, and well versed in the latest building techniques. A thoughtful, strong, and trustworthy man, Marcus was trained in his father's trade and has lived a simple life in Port Haven for many years.

Well respected in town, he has raised a happy family, all of whom have survived the storm. You know that he was deeply shocked by seeing the fishermen swept away. Even so, you are heartened to see that, among all the dejected faces of those who sit on or wander across the hillside, Marcus's appears optimistic, even cheerful.

"Marcus," you say as you approach him, "how can you seem in such good spirits?"

"Oh, my friend," the curly-haired man sighs, sitting himself down achingly upon the remains of a barrel, "we must put forth the effort in times such as these to keep our spirits alight, otherwise there is nothing but despair."

He looks up at you, and now you see the deep lines of weariness around his eyes. Like everybody else, he has not slept, but his smile remains unforced. "Yes, my friend," he tells you firmly, "we have lost our homes and every twig of everything else, so we must start anew. But there is cause for joy in this, for there is great satisfaction in building afresh. From the humblest washtub to the highest rooftop, I'll build you a better town than this last."

"Marcus," you reply, a smile widening on your own face, "we will need your skills and your attitude to survive. I am glad to call you my friend."

Marcus Wainwright

"Just keep me and my apprentices fed, and tell me what you want and where you want it. We'll build you a nice new town we can all be proud to live in and call home. You'll see!"

Josephine Fletcher, Archer, Hunter, Trapper

Josephine Fletcher, the gifted daughter of an old poacher, has learned her father's trade well. She is an expert trapper, ever able to elude the authorities while hunting on crown lands. She is equally skilled in hunting with a bow. In fact, she has become a legend in Port Haven for performing the archer's trick of splitting one arrow with another. Her fiery spirit is also well known.

Poachers

In medieval England, the wealthy and powerful considered the wild game animals of England, such as deer, to be for their tables alone; they outlawed hunting among the common people. In such lean times as the 1400s, this law was difficult to obey, and thus illegal hunters, called poachers, became common.

Josephine Fletcher

"What is it you have come to ask me, Jo?" you inquire as the tall young woman approaches. Among the bedraggled survivors, Josephine alone appears calm and unaffected, her soft leather boots stepping lightly on the muddy hillside. Living in the wood has taught her grace in adverse circumstances. Josephine would make a formidable ally in your quest.

"I see how you are assembling Port Haven's most talented to keep us all alive," she says with a note of determination. "Well, I am here to say you'll be needing me too!"

I know it, you think, but you decide to let her explain herself.

"Aye," she goes on, "one buck can feed a mob like ours for a week, and I can teach you how to bring one down and never be seen at the task. I can trap both beast and fowl, and I can train dogs and horses, for I have an understanding with animals. I've spent my life studying the ways of the forest and its creatures. And you know that if I'm needed to loose my arrows on two-legged beasts, I can do that too!" She has spoken firmly but now looks at you uncertainly, and each of you knows why.

You both cast your gaze over the gathered people. Josephine has always lived apart from the town, as though she were herself part wild. When she was thought of at all, the people spoke of her using the tones of contempt reserved for those who are different, and with the note of fear inspired by those who are strong. Josephine is both.

At length you sigh and shake your head. "Never you mind," you tell her. "If I say you are to be trusted, then they will accept it. Before long, everybody will understand exactly how much they need you."

Josephine chortles at this and says, "I always hoped that one day they'd offer me some respect!"

Red-Handed

The penalty for being caught in the crime of poaching was often death. The expression "caught red-handed" originated in the medieval period. The red referred to blood on the hands of the criminal.

Albos Black, Blacksmith

Even at the age of three, Albos found himself drawn to the smithy. He would stand gazing in wonder at the sparks and the blast of steam as the blacksmith dipped red-hot metal. He grew up an eager apprentice and eventually took on the tasks himself with hearty skill.

Built of solid muscle from his ankles up, Albos is a stocky man with a round face and a spectacular beard. "Thick, so the sparks can't reach my cheeks!" he likes to laugh.

You have often watched him work, chatting cheerfully about his trade. "My father wanted me to go with him to the fishing, but I couldn't resist the *tink-tink* call of the hammers, the smell of sparks and hot metal, so down to the smithy I trailed."

Albos works with bog iron collected from the iron-rich peat lands of England, heating and hammering it into tools, weapons, armor, and other valued hardware. As well as this, he has kept the Port Haven armory well equipped with many hundreds of war arrowheads and blades.

It is a fortunate thing, you reflect, that Albos has lived

Albos Black

Metal and Magic

Medieval society had a limited understanding of science and a deep respect for superstition. The physical world was understood in terms of the four elements: earth, fire, air, and water. The blacksmith worked with all four of these elements: he drew metal from the earth, he fanned the fire with air from the bellows, and he cooled hot metal in water. Many people considered this the work of a sort of magician. For this reason, the blacksmith was often called upon to cast away dark spirits and even to perform marriages.

through the storm. Without a blacksmith, your people would be hard-pressed to survive long in the world. Albos is definitely the next person you want to see this morning …

"Ho, there! What a grim day," Albos cries in greeting, his round, red face dour. "My smithy is destroyed. Only the anvil and a few of my tools survived. We are ruined!"

"That may not be quite so," you say encouragingly. "Marcus seems glad enough to think of building a new town. A town inland, Albos— think of that. Away from this cold and deadly sea."

The blacksmith glowers at his feet. "Do you really believe it?"

"I do," you assure him. "And I need you to believe it as well. You are one of the great pins that holds our community together, and I'll not leave you to sink into despair. I need you to lend me your strength. To help us rebuild!"

Albos Black thinks a long moment and then looks you in the eye. "If you say it can be done, then I'll believe it. I suppose a new town would be well served by my forge and hammers. I could make all manner of everything you need, from nails and hinges to pots and weapons." He grins suddenly at the thought of it.

"I'll build and run a new smithy, wherever we end up!" he declares, slapping you heartily on the back.

Deborah Cobbler, shoemaker, leather and cord worker

Deborah's love of her father, who was a gifted leather worker, grew into a passion for his craft. But she also loved animals, and it took a long time for her to accept that making leather meant taking the lives of cows for their skins. Now, after many years, she explains her beliefs this way: "To work well is to work in awareness. I wake every sunrise to sing a private song of thanks to the beasts. Every shoe to the smallest thread is made with my knowing and my song."

Deborah is an expert in preparing raw animal skins and working them into useful items. From leather she makes ropes and clothes, writing surfaces, tools, and, of course, shoes. You will need her if any new settlement is to be successful.

"There you are, Deborah," you say to the tall, middle-aged woman upon finding her at last. She is still picking through the remains of her old workshop. "I am glad to see you survived the night."

"Aye, that makes two of us. But the storm has washed away all of my efforts!" Ruefully, she

Deborah Cobbler

pushes a strand of graying hair from her face and looks around the remains of her old workshop. "Shoes have laces, but who ever would have thought I should have used them to moor my work to prevent it being carried off in a flood?" She turns to crack a grin at you. This is a good sign.

"Deb, we are planning a quest for a new site to rebuild. A new town, but inland. Away from the sea."

"Aye." She nods again. "We have all feared that someday it must be so. Until now, though, we were all too comfortable to consider such frightening thoughts. All but you. How long have you been planning this?"

"I've been thinking about it for a couple of years now," you admit. "As a precaution."

"Always looking out for the rest of us, you are." She sighs deeply, surveying the mud and broken timber. "Is it a good plan you have?"

"The best I could muster up. But it is worth little without you. We can't walk or work without shoes on our feet. Or without ropes and horn, or the hundred other things you alone have the ability to make so well."

"Aye," Deborah says thoughtfully. Then she slaps her hands together with finality. "So I take it that you've already talked to Sir Greggor Knight, old Mirriam Wise, Marcus Wainwright the woodman, huntress Josephine, and good Albos Black with his forge?"

You blink at her. "Yes. Each one of them. You've done some thinking as well, I see."

Deborah laughs. "Indeed. But you're the one for the leader's job. Who would want to follow a tanner? I stink too much from my work!" She waves her hand before you can protest. "I'll gather my kit and goods. When do we set off?"

You are the seventh expert, the one in charge of all the others.

As a leader, you have to be an expert in the art of keeping a group of people organized and enthusiastic. This is not a simple thing. Your band of survivors and the six experts will bring all their problems and final decisions to you, seeking smart answers and support.

The collected knowledge of these experts is listed in the Experts' Catalog at the back of this book (starting on page 72), which is divided into six categories, one for each of the elders. You will need their wisdom to survive the coming days.

Good luck!

YEAR ONE
The New Land

ONE MONTH HAS PASSED SINCE THE STORM. AFTER THREE WEEKS OF difficult travel, of fighting hunger, rains, and bandits, your people are at last blessed with clear weather and a happy discovery: you have come upon a beautiful valley. In front of you are rolling meadows of clover with a river running through them. Farther off, you can see a huge and ancient wood. It seems the perfect land to settle upon.

But something is not quite right. A short distance into the lush valley, you discover the ravaged remains of a previous settlement, the stones blackened by fire. The destruction, Sir Greggor reports, appears to be less than a year old.

"Brr! This is not uncommon," Sir Greggor huffs through his mustache. "The local lords are forever at war in these parts. They send their soldiers to burn down each other's villages while they themselves hide safe in their keeps and castles. It is brutal and endless, and it makes me furious!"

"But we are deep in the Border Marches," Albos points out. "Nobody can truly claim ownership of this land, and the nearest lordships are far away."

"Would you build another town upon these ruins?" you ask with surprise. "This valley is otherwise perfect, but I am given pause.

The Black Death

The Black Death, or the Plague, was an illness that ravaged Europe, killing approximately one-quarter of its population. Originating in Asia, the epidemic followed trade routes, moving westward into continental Europe in 1347, and then traveling to England in 1348. England had an estimated population of 3.7 million when the Black Death first struck. Sixty years later, only 2.1 million people remained.

STARVATION AND DISEASE

Inexplicably, some communities suffered severe losses while others did not. However, in general, the poor, the elderly, and communities suffering from poor crop harvests were the most vulnerable. Starvation after poor harvests weakened immune systems, and this was the worst time for the Plague to strike.

SPOTS AND SNEEZES

The Plague was in fact two forms of the same disease: the *Bubonic Plague*, carried by rats and transmitted to humans through flea bites, and the *Pneumonic Plague*, spread by coughing or sneezing. People who caught the Plague suffered from burning sensations in the throat and lungs, stabbing pains in the chest, vomiting of blood, strange growths in the armpits and upon the groin and neck, and purple or black spots across the skin.

STRANGE CURES

With limited understanding of medical science, people of the Middle Ages attempted cures for the Black Death that were often peculiar, although some came close to making sense in modern terms. "Cures" included bleeding subjects (opening veins to release the disease), diets of fruits and vegetables (in the belief that foods, like meat, that rot and smell bad caused the disease), washing victims in vinegar and rose water, burning incense, and stirring the air that had "grown thick" (by ringing bells or shooting guns outdoors).

EXTREME SOLUTIONS

In Milan, Italy, victims' houses were walled up, even if this meant trapping healthy family members inside. This drastic measure seemed to pay off, as Milan lost less than 15 percent of its population during the Plague, the lowest death rate in all of Italy.

I do not wish our people to suffer the same fate as those before us."

"Well now, let's not let our fears get ahead of us," Sir Greggor cautions. "It is true that this blackened stone casts a long shadow on the imagination. In fairness, though, I can see no sign of defensive structures. Not even a simple watchtower. Whoever lived here—they were not prepared for trouble."

You study his face intently. "Do you think, if we settled here, we could adequately protect ourselves?"

Sir Greggor squints at the land for a long moment, surveying and then nodding firmly. "Even the shape of the hillsides and the lay of the river lend themselves well to defense. I don't know everything that those before us were lacking, but tactical planning seems chief among them. And I can show any would-be town burners a new trick or two. We should build here. That's my advice."

Mirriam had wandered some distance, bending and examining the surrounding plants. Now she returns and listens with sharp attention. "I agree," she says. "All places will have their danger, but not everywhere is as fine as this. Why, there are useful herbs as far as the eye can see!"

"And that river and those mighty woods," murmurs Josephine, gazing in rapture. "Almost untouched! We'll be fed well on all manner of beast, fish, and bird if we stay here."

"I'll be able to run a good blacksmith shop and forge here," says Albos. "Back half a league or so, we passed not far from a good source of bog iron and a good trading road, too."

All the others agree as well. You can see hope glowing on their faces.

"Very good, then," you declare, a weight lifting from your chest. You have not had cause to feel the relief of hope in many days. "This shall be our new home. New Haven!"

Year One Instructions

Winter is only six months away. Your people are weary from travel and you have little food in your reserves. If you do not build shelters and find enough to eat, you may not survive the cold months. As the leader of your people, it is your duty to decide how best to make use of the limited supplies you have available.

Step 1. Year Beginning Scores

Effort: **1,000**   *Supplies:* **100**   *Defense:* **0**

Add these scores to your score chart now.

Step 2. Random Events

Roll a six-sided die. If you roll:

1, 2, or 3: You find a hidden cache of tools! Add 50 to your Supplies score.

4, 5, or 6: No random events this year.

Step 3. Goals

Year One Goal: *Supplies* must reach at least 1,000.

Turn to the Experts' Catalog (starting on page 72) now and choose your Actions and Projects. Remember, your *Effort* points will not carry over into next year, so spend them all if you can!

When your *Supplies* have reached 1,000 or more, continue to Step 4. If you are unable to reach a *Supplies* score of 1,000, turn to page 71.

Step 4. Year One Completion and Bonuses

Good work! You have managed to keep your people alive and fed for the first year. Their hard work has paid off and they are grateful to you for your leadership.

Bonus For every *Supplies* point you managed to gain above your Goal, give yourself +1 *Effort* point. (For example, a *Supplies* score of 1,225 adds 225 *Effort*.) Add this Bonus to Step 1 in Year Two.

YEAR TWO
Bread and Fish

WITH AN EARTHY RELEASE, THE TREE-BRANCH PLOW BURSTS awkwardly from the soil. The six men pulling upon its ropes stagger forward, barely catching themselves from sprawling to the ground.

"Augh! This is right rough work you've got us at, Mirriam!" the foremost of them complains, rubbing his hands together in the cold of the early spring. "We'll be battered to bits before the first seeds are ever planted if you keep us at it like this."

It is true. Port Haveners know how to pull a fish from the ocean and gut it faster than a man can wink, but farming is another world to them.

Mirriam Wise only shakes her head at him and wags her finger. "Farming is not so difficult. It's this packed earth that's the trouble." She surveys the dozen hungry fishermen who have volunteered to break up and prepare the resilient ground, pocked and tufted with rocks and weeds, to receive the precious seeds. "Pick up the plow. Try again."

Despite the poor show, Mirriam turns to you brightly, clearly bubbling with excitement over the project. "Isn't it wonderful?" she crows, her breath coming in misty puffs in the bright chill of the morning. "Not just a little vegetable patch as I've had in the past, but a proper field! I've always saved seeds every year from my favorite plants. As you know, my childhood wasn't spent cutting fish, but on a farm. I remember everything my mother taught me. It's very lucky that enough seeds survived the storm to plant with."

"Lucky indeed," you agree as you observe the hopeful industry. There are other men picking at the ground with roughly fashioned hoes, trying to break up the knotted soil. Mirriam can see the doubtful squint in your eye as you watch them.

"We need a better plow and a healthy pair of beasts to pull it," she admits, "if we are to do it properly. I am not certain our boys will be able to till this ground enough for planting a field as big as we need. But some is better than nothing at all."

"Keep at it, Mirriam. Albos promises me he has the solution," you reassure her before heading off to see Albos Black at his makeshift forge.

"Aha!" the forge master booms, seeing you approach the little clearing he has made into his workplace. "I've got something to show you, my friend. Come take a look!" Albos stands over the prized object. "It will be finished soon!"

"It is a plow head," you observe. "But it looks not like any plow I have seen."

"It is not! It is better. I have heard tell of such an innovation in the south and decided to try building one for Mirriam. See here." He indicates the plow's long wooden tooth meant to tear through earth, but his has been fitted with a beaten metal plate. "The ground here is packed hard, and wood alone is simply a poor tool for cutting and turning the earth," he explains. "And so, I have sheathed it in metal!

See how I've hammered it into an edge? This will make the work of plowing much easier!"

Your eyes brighten as you grasp the elegance of the device. You nod to the proud blacksmith. "I think Mirriam will be very pleased with this."

"It will work. You'll see!" Albos smiles widely. "Our food problems will soon be a thing of the past."

You move onward, encouraged by Albos's enthusiasm but still troubled. Even if the new plow works, it will still take many weeks before the fields will produce food. Plants do not flourish overnight, and the people are hungry now. You sigh darkly as you move on to survey another vital project.

As you approach the river, you see a gathering of serious-faced fishermen all watching with rapt interest a nettle-hemp fishing line tug and then jerk. It cuts into the thin crust of river ice, not yet fully melted. The watchers all crane their necks to see. With an expert yank of her wrist, Josephine Fletcher pulls a large fish from the river, the cord and fishing hook caught soundly in its mouth. The silver creature flickers through the air to slap and flop upon the pebbles. A sharp crack with a haft of wood and the fish is dead. All those assembled make noises of approval.

"This little river is flowing well with fish," Jo reports to her audience. "But this is no way to feed a town. All of you have been surviving on our few rescued stores from last year, and on the bucks and hares I've been poaching. We'll starve unless I can teach you how to angle halfway right in this freshwater. But I'm betting I can't."

Many in her audience go red in their cheeks and look down.

"Stop your gloating, Jo," you say, approaching the riverside. She greets you with a wicked eye cast up from where she is crouched. Then, seeing the firmness behind your smile, she gives way.

Learning a Trade

If a teenager was to learn a craft, he or she would become an *apprentice* to a *master* in one of the crafts, such as leather working or blacksmithing. Teens did not often have a choice as to which craft they would enter or who would be their master. Typically, family connections determined which trades were available.

Getting Paid

An apprentice worked for no pay, living with a master of a craft for anywhere from 2 to 10 years before graduating to the rank of *journeyman*. A journeyman could then work for pay under any master offering employment. To become a master, the journeyman needed to submit an example of work to the *trade guild*, an organization made up of masters of the craft. If accepted, the new master could start a business and train apprentices.

"I do beg your pardon," she says to the abashed fishermen, standing up. "You will pick up these freshwater skills soon enough—so long as I am teaching you. And so long as our cordwright can produce enough line for us … and perhaps even some nets to replace those lost in the storm."

You all cast a glance at another of your experts, who stands upon the river's edge this morning.

"Well, don't look at me like that. I'm weaving as fast as I can," Deborah Cobbler retorts. "And my apprentice, too. But it's slow work. The best I can do will be to equip perhaps half of you with fishing lines by summer. You want nets? That takes fifty times the cord and that much work again in weaving. Help me pull the hemp and treat and spin it, why not?"

"Just keep at it, my friends," you encourage them. "We're clever enough to solve this."

With Mirriam's work and Albos's new plow, and the river promising a rich supply of fish, you feel a cautious flame of confidence sparking within. The sun grows higher in the sky, bathing the valley in warmth.

"Well, with luck it will be enough," you say to yourself. "We've all spring and summer to see that it is."

Year Two Instructions

You must feed your people. Spend your resource points wisely to ensure a steady food supply.

Step 1: Year Beginning Scores

Effort: **1,000** (plus any Bonuses from Year One, Step 4)
Supplies: **–500** (because food has been eaten and firewood has been used)
Check your Permanent Items chart. Add any Yearly Bonuses to your scores now.

Step 2: Random Events

Use the Random Events chart on page 96.

Step 3: Goals

Year Two Goal: *Supplies* must reach at least 1,200 before you continue to Step 4.
Choose your Actions and Projects now.
If you are unable to reach a *Supplies* score of 1,200, turn to page 71.

Step 4: Year Two Completion and Bonuses

Good work! You have managed to keep your people alive and fed for another year!

Bonus For every *Supplies* point you managed to gain above your Goal, give yourself +1 *Effort* point. (For example, a *Supplies* score of 1,425 adds 225 *Effort*.) Add this Bonus to Step 1 in Year Three.

YEAR THREE
The Tinkers

"COME QUICK!" THE YOUNG LOOKOUT GASPS UPON FINDING YOU. He is out of breath after running from the perch built into the tall elm tree at the edge of the valley. "More people! More people have come!"

You and the boy race along the footpath to find that, indeed, a ragtag gathering of men and women has arrived in a small clearing where the path emerges from the woods and into view of the village.

The newcomers, about 50 of them in all, stand warily near their travel gear, pots, and packs. Their clothes are made of worn leather and many wear straw hats upon weathered brows. They have arrived with some hand-pulled carts and two donkeys, all laden with an odd collection of goods: cloths and tins and bottles and greased leather packages wrapped tight in string. Your own people have dropped their morning tasks to investigate the alarm, and now they are gathered to watch.

It is clear from their faces that they are fascinated, but they keep safely behind Sir Greggor. He is standing with his hands on his hips and his cheeks puffed up.

"Oh no, you don't!" he booms. "No further!"

"Ah, we have visitors," you observe loudly so that all can hear. "I hope we have been treating them kindly. We have no need of trouble."

"Tinkers," Sir Greggor sighs heavily, as though an old problem never solved has risen once again to trouble his thoughts. "They are men and women like us, but the tinkers' reputation for thievery and trickery is well known. Be it fair or not, I am concerned for our supplies and stores should this lot prove untrustworthy. It might be best if we sent them on their way."

The Nomad Tinkers

Tinkers were nomadic people. They had no land, answered to no lord, and paid no taxes. They traveled in groups, trading and selling their simple repair and labor services in order to survive. Tinkers were often distrusted in 14th-century England, considered little better than beggars, people who might cheat you if they could. Despite this, they were somewhat tolerated as they provided useful services.

Tin and Lead

Tin is a soft metal that could not be repaired with a blacksmith's heavy tools and the much higher temperatures necessary to forge iron. The name *tinker* probably came from the Middle English word *tinkere*, meaning "tin worker." Tinkers used solder, a mixture of tin and molten lead, to fill holes in tin buckets and pots.

A wiry man with a crinkly face and dust from the road upon his clothes steps up to address you. "Please pardon our intrusion. It is true that we are tinkers, but trouble we are not. We've come looking to trade our wares, for we have many interesting things you and your people may need."

Everybody—tinkers, Sir Greggor, and all the people of New Haven—looks at you to hear what you will say.

You can do one of two things:

1. Turn the tinkers away. If you choose this option, the tinkers move on. Continue to the next page.

2. Let them stay. If you decide to welcome the tinkers, then turn to the Trade and Tinker chart on page 96 to see what happens. When you are done, come back to this page and continue.

News by Road and Sea

Trade in medieval England occurred along well-traveled roads and shipping lines. As tinkers traveled these roads regularly, they often became the only source of trade for villages, such as New Haven, that were off the beaten path. The news and stories from far away carried by tinkers were also valued, and thus tinkers earned a degree of grudging respect.

Peasants and Serfs

Peasants and serfs made up the largest social group in medieval England, representing approximately 90 percent of the population. Peasants had a limited freedom, and they paid taxes and rent to their landlords by way of coin and goods. Serfs were little better than slaves who worked the land for the lords and were allowed to keep a small portion of their product to feed and shelter themselves. Both peasants and serfs were considered the property of the lord whose lands they occupied. They were restricted from moving to another location or working for another lord.

Year Three Instructions

Step 1: Year Beginning Scores
Effort: **1,200 (plus any Bonuses from last year)**
Supplies: **–600 (food has been eaten; firewood has been used)**
Check your Permanent Items chart. Add any Yearly Bonuses to your scores now.

Step 2: Random Events
Use the Random Events chart on page 96.

Step 3: Goals
Year Three Goal: *Supplies* **must reach at least 1,200 before you continue to Step 4.**
Choose your Actions and Projects now.
If you are unable to reach a *Supplies* score of 1,200, turn to page 71.

Step 4: Year Three Completion and Bonuses
Good work! You have managed to keep your people alive and fed for another year!

Bonus For every *Supplies* point you managed to gain above your Goal, give yourself +1 *Effort* point. (For example, a *Supplies* score of 1,425 adds 225 *Effort*.) Add this Bonus to Step 1 in Year Four.

YEAR FOUR
The Earl

STONES BITE SHARPLY INTO YOUR KNEES AS YOU CROUCH, HIDDEN among the bushes, at the foot of a broad oak. The lungful of air in your chest burns and you realize that you have been holding it for a long time. As you let it out, you become aware of the distant drumming of hooves. In another minute you can make out voices coming toward you through the woods.

"That's them," Sir Greggor rumbles softly at your side. Then he raises his voice enough to be heard by the other villagers you have brought with you, who have hidden themselves on either side of the trail. There are five in all, including Josephine, your deadliest shot with a longbow. "Ready yourselves," Greggor says, "but keep your heads down and your wits about you. We have the advantage here, so stay calm."

The riders break over the ridge and come into view. They slow their beasts to a walk, chain mail and swords clanking.

Sir Greggor squints at the mystery riders and then speaks into your ear. "That merchant told us true. I count eight.

Death and Taxes

In medieval England, people living on a ruler's land were called *peasants*, and they were required to pay a tax to the landowner. The tax, which applied to every person over the age of 13, amounted to 10 percent of each peasant's yearly income, or the equivalent value in grain and produce. This tax was called a *tithe*, from the Old English word *teogotha*, meaning "a tenth." The tithe was a heavy burden for peasants, and it often made the difference between starvation and survival.

Armed with swords and crossbows. Light armor. Leather and some chain mail. We were fortunate to have had forewarning enough to prepare."

"Those riders can be plucked off easily enough," Josephine whispers. She is crouched by your other side, her eyes alight. She has been involved in this sort of dangerous adventure before, having had to risk her life evading authorities.

"Not so quick, now," you caution both of them. "Remember what we are here to do. I shall meet them peacefully first to see what their business is. But Josephine, you and your archers stay hidden in case there is trouble."

"Aye, I'll do that," she says with a wink, notching an arrow upon the string of her longbow.

The riders are now very close. You heave yourself to your feet so that you are in plain view beside the oak tree, ready to vanish behind it in an instant should things turn ugly. In the most commanding voice you can muster, you bellow,

Tithes to the King

Landowners in turn paid tithes to the king. After so many peasants lost their lives to the Black Death, landowners could not find enough workers to grow the crops they needed in order to pay their own tithes to the king. The surviving peasants, now in high demand, were in a position to seek other landowners who might tax them less. The ruling class, frightened by this prospect, immediately passed laws that made it illegal for workers to leave their landowners or to seek a higher value for their products and work.

Wat Tyler and the Peasants' Revolt

In 1381, King Richard II introduced a new tax. Every person in England, whether rich or poor, was to pay a tax of 12 pence. Of course, this tax weighed most heavily on poorer people, including peasants, who were already struggling. A blacksmith named Wat Tyler was outraged when a tax collector stripped his daughter naked to determine whether she was old enough to pay the tax. Tyler smashed the man's head with a hammer, killing him. He quickly became a popular hero and leader of a revolt.

When Wat Tyler marched on London with an army of 100,000 peasants, soldiers, and clergy, King Richard promised to meet all their demands. However, London's mayor, who was present at the meeting between the King and the rebel leaders, attacked Tyler, severely wounding him. The tide turned and the revolt fell apart. The revolutionists fell into disarray and withdrew to their homes, and Tyler was put to death. The King broke his promise, hunting down and hanging 1,500 of the rebels.

"Ho there, riders! You are entering the settlement of New Haven! Explain your business!"

The riders, who all appear to be middle-aged professional soldiers, react immediately, raising their crossbows to scan the dense wood around them. You can see the alarm in their faces as they spot you but continue to look for others. They know it is not a good place to be caught in an ambush.

Their leader is a broad-bellied, pockmarked man with a black helmet strapped to his skull. He narrows his eyes at you, and two of his men aim crossbows at your chest with grim intention.

"You speak boldly for a squatter!" he bellows back. "I represent my lord, the Earl of Cheshire, to whom this land rightly belongs. It has come to his knowledge that a group of vagabonds has settled upon his land, and now we have come to sort you out. The Earl will allow you to stay, but you must pay him in order to live upon his land. Payment must be made every year, and it can be taken in crops, livestock, or any money you happen to have. The first payment is due immediately. If you refuse this offer, we will drive you and your people from your homes. Any who try to stop us will be executed on the spot!"

Greggor frowns and hisses into your ear. "Blast it. The Earl is a blackguard. I know of his work! He has razed villages larger than ours. These threats are not the sort we can ignore."

The Earl's captain rises boldly in his saddle and juts his fierce jaw at you. "What say you?"

You can do one of two things:
1. Refuse to comply with the Earl's demands.
2. Agree to pay tax to the Earl of Cheshire.

1. Refuse to comply with the Earl's demands.

"Never," you cry. "Your earl will collect no taxes here! Turn around and leave at once, or you shall be driven off!"

One of the soldiers sneers at you and raises his crossbow, but Josephine, in her secret perch, is faster. She shoots the man dead, and her archers send a flurry of arrows into the riders' midst. In the confusion, you and Sir Greggor spring your trap.

You are now at war with the Earl of Cheshire. Turn to the Battle chart on page 96 to see what happens. When you are done, continue to Year Four Instructions on the next page.

2. Agree to pay tax to the Earl of Cheshire.

Wanting to avoid war, you agree to comply with the Earl's demands. With long faces and much grumbling, your people give up their hard-won goods and crops to the soldiers. The Earl of Cheshire is now your lord. It is his obligation to protect your people from aggressors.

Your Defense score is immediately reduced to 0. You are not allowed to arm yourselves or build any structures that will add to your Defense score in the future.

You will have to make tax payments. The tax is half of your Supplies score. Subtract that now as the Earl's soldiers carry away the best of New Haven's food and resources. The Earl's tax collectors will return at least once every year for this purpose, but may do so more often if they please.

Year Four Instructions

Step 1: Year Beginning Scores
Effort: 1,400 (plus any Bonuses from last year; also, subtract any Deductions caused by losses from battle this year)
Supplies: −600 (also, subtract any Deductions caused by losses from battle this year)

Check your Permanent Items chart. Add any Yearly Bonuses to your scores now.

If you welcomed the tinkers last year and had good dealings with them, then they will return this year. You may choose now to spend 400 from *Supplies* in order to add 600 to this year's *Effort* score.

Step 2: Random Events
Use the Random Events chart on page 96.

Step 3: Goals
Year Four Goal: *Supplies* must reach at least 1,500 before you continue to Step 4.

Choose your Actions and Projects now.

If you are unable to reach a *Supplies* score of 1,500, turn to page 71.

Step 4: Year Four Completion and Bonuses
Good work! You have managed to keep your people alive and fed for another year!

Bonus For every *Supplies* point you managed to gain above your Goal, give yourself +1 *Effort* point. (For example, a *Supplies* score of 1,725 adds 225 *Effort*.) Add this Bonus to Step 1 in Year Five.

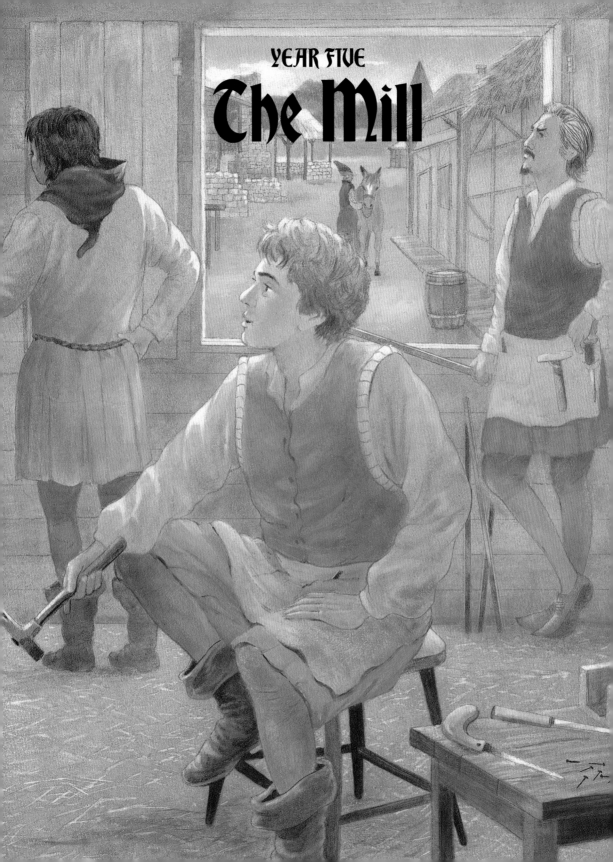

YEAR FIVE
The Mill

IT IS SPRINGTIME AGAIN IN NEW HAVEN. THE FRESH BREEZE OF A new season is wafting through your community, and everyone is buzzing with energy. Today, however, their excitement has taken an angry turn. A brightly clad messenger, with tassels bouncing on his silver-trimmed coat, arrived this morning with a message, then departed again without a word upon its delivery. You begin to read the message aloud to several villagers who have gathered, and the effect on them is explosive.

"Now the Earl wants us to build a *mill*?" Marcus exclaims in disgust. "It sounds rotten to me. He's utterly untrustworthy!"

You continue reading from the large piece of parchment. "He is ordering that we dam the river and build a mill. At our own expense. The water wheel is to turn a great millstone for grinding grain. A millwright is being sent to direct its construction."

The villagers burst into angry, excited chatter.

MULCURE, the Flour Cax

In the Middle Ages, the mill and the village of Houghton Mill (between modern-day Cambridge and Peterborough) were owned by the great Benedictine abbey of Ramsey, 16 kilometers (10 miles) from Houghton. All the villagers worked for the abbey, growing crops and tending livestock. Villagers had to grind their corn in the abbey's mill or pay a heavy fine. The abbey then claimed a proportion of the flour, usually one-seventeenth, in a tax known as *multure*.

Deborah Cobbler stands thoughtfully for a moment, gazing up the river, before at last speaking. "Grinding by hand, as we do now, is hard work. A mill would make flour production a thing of ease. And you, Marcus, could learn a great deal from this millwright fellow."

"But it's the *Earl*, Deborah!" Marcus protests. "We can never trust that man!"

"Well, think now," she replies mildly. "It has not been all bad. Some of us have done well by his lordship."

"*Some* of us have been making boots for his household!" Marcus retorts accusingly.

Deborah nods without embarrassment. "Yes, I've turned a tidy profit. It is wealth that I am able to pass on to others in our community. I think that building a mill can bring us further good fortune. It will give our folk more time for other tasks."

"The Earl is in a sorry position," you reflect aloud. "With the plague having killed so many, the landlords have fewer

Dodging Multure

Villagers tried to avoid multure by grinding their own corn or by taking it to a mill with a lower charge. In 1310, Richard Plombe of Houghton was fined six pence for having his corn ground in the wrong mill. This was a large sum, for the average daily wage at the time was only one or two pence. People could avoid paying the multure tax altogether by grinding grain in their homes, using small grindstones, also called *querns*.

Paved with Grindstones

In 1330, Richard of Wallingford, abbot of the monastery of St. Albans, sent the sheriff to search for and confiscate all home grindstones. Richard used the stones to pave the courtyard of the abbey's cloister. During the great Peasants' Revolt of 1381, led by Wat Tyler, the peasants stormed the monastery and broke up the courtyard to reclaim the grindstones.

willing hands. You too, Marcus, could have profited from his lordship, I hear—had you chosen to."

Marcus's frown deepens. "I'll not coop barrels for that schemer, no matter what he offers."

You sigh pensively. "This turn does indeed worry me." Everybody around you grows quiet to listen. "I have heard of mills being built in other places, and there is a hidden price. When the work is done, the Earl will consider the mill to be his own possession. We will have to pay if we want to use it."

Marcus gives a short laugh. "He'll have a hard time with that. Money is already scarce. People have little enough as it is without having to *pay* for flour as well as the grain to make it! We will simply continue to grind flour for ourselves, and his mill can go rot!"

You shake your head. "Well, that's the trick of it. There is a chance that the Earl may outlaw manual grinders. I've heard tell of this from other parts—the sheriff goes with his men to each household and they smash all the small grindstones. That way, we must all pay for something that, up until now, has been free. It will make him even wealthier and us poorer."

"But …" says Deborah, ever thoughtful. "If we are freed from having to grind flour ourselves, we would have more time in our days. We could spend that time at more fruitful labors, and thus we could afford to buy flour, as well as other things."

"No, Deborah!" Marcus shakes his head in fury. "No! I would build and use a water mill, but on my own terms— for our people, *not* because it is a law that will make the Earl richer still."

"Clearly," you say, raising your hand to hold attention, "we must think wisely on this before we choose our actions. If we do not build this mill for the Earl as he instructs, it will mean facing more of his troops …"

Year Five Instructions

If you are at war with the Earl of Cheshire, he attacks this year. If you surrender, reduce your *Defense* score to 0, go to Step 1, and pay taxes to the Earl. If you resist, turn to the Battle chart on page 96 to determine what happens.

Step 1: Year Beginning Scores

Effort: 1,400 (plus or minus any Bonuses or Deductions)

Supplies: –1,000 (plus or minus any Bonuses or Deductions)

Check your Permanent Items chart. Add any Yearly Bonuses to your scores now.

● If you have welcomed the tinkers in the past and had good dealings with them, they will return this year. You may choose now to spend 600 from *Supplies* in order to add 600 to this year's *Effort* score.

● If you pay taxes to the Earl of Cheshire, subtract one-half of your *Supplies* score now.

● If you want to rebel against the Earl, you may choose Actions and Projects to increase your Defense score this year. In Year Six, you will be at war with the Earl.

Step 2: Random Events

Use the Random Events chart on page 96.

Step 3: Goals

Year Five Goal: *Supplies* must reach at least 1,500 before you continue to Step 4.

● You may attempt to build either a horizontal water mill or a vertical water mill starting this year (see page 83).

Choose your Actions and Projects now.

If you are unable to reach a *Supplies* score of 1,500, turn to page 71.

Step 4: Year Five Completion and Bonuses

Bonus For every *Supplies* point you managed to gain above your Goal, give yourself +1 *Effort* point. (For example, a *Supplies* score of 1,725 adds 225 *Effort*.) Add this Bonus to Step 1 in Year Six.

YEAR SIX

The Duke

AFTER SIX YEARS, NEW HAVEN HAS PUT DOWN SOME ROOTS IN THE valley. More buildings have been constructed; fields of young crops extend farther into the valley; and children born in the community are now playing in the yards and in the town square. You and your trusted friends have dealt as well as you can with the Earl's demands. But suddenly a new foe, completely unexpected, threatens …

All are dazed as a shrill cry carries through the town: "Soldiers! Soldiers! Horsemen and soldiers!"

You race to the tallest structure at the edge of New Haven. There is a boy at the top, scanning the horizon. Everyone cranes their necks up at him, bodies tensed for danger. "Is it the Earl's men?" you call up to him. "How many?"

The boy squints. "A dozen horsemen and soldiers," he cries. "They have swords and crossbows. And flaming sticks! I don't know who they are."

"To arms!" you command, pushing your stunned friends

Rain of Stone

While the men were engaged in direct combat, the women were often left to run the catapults. In 1218, during the siege of Toulouse, Simon de Montfort, the feared leader of the crusade against heretical Albigensians, was struck on the head and killed in battle by a stone catapulted by the town women.

Protected by Water

The medieval coastal town of Yarmouth used a unique system of defensive moats that were based on semi-natural formations in the land. These helped repel invaders through the 12th and 13th centuries. Fearing a French invasion, King Henry VIII had a castle built there in 1547. In 1662, a moat was cut around the eastern end of the town. Secured by a drawbridge and a permanent garrison of troops, Yarmouth became one of the best-defended towns in England.

and neighbors to their posts. It has been quiet all winter, and they seem slow to remember that such danger must be met quickly or all could be lost. Within a moment, people are scurrying for weapons and cover.

"Go! Quickly!" you yell. "We must defend ourselves!"

Turn to the Battle chart on page 96 to determine what happens next.

"Who were they?" gasp the people as they emerge from cover, breathless and shaken.

"They serve the Duke of Pettyham," growls Sir Greggor, his face blackened in the battle. "The Duke is an old enemy of the Earl's. Because we are on the Earl's land, he believes that attacking us will do his enemy harm. These warlord nobility are a filthy lot, and here we are, honest people, caught in the middle!"

"Indeed," you agree, your face grim. "It is time something was done!"

The Long Wall

In 898, the town of Wallingford was part of an elaborate defense system known as the Burghal Hidage, an extensive series of small forts spanning an entire region. Each fort was made the responsibility of a local landowning family, with each family supplying its fort with one soldier. At its height, Wallingford had a defensive force of 2,400 men, who could defend a circuit 3,000 meters (3,300 yards) in circumference.

Year Six Instructions

If you are at war with the Earl of Cheshire, he also attacks this year. If you surrender, reduce your *Defense* score to 0, go to Step 1, and pay taxes to the Earl. If you resist, turn to the Battle chart on page 96 to determine what happens.

Step 1: Year Beginning Scores

Effort: 1,400 (plus or minus any Bonuses or Deductions)
Supplies: –1,000 (plus or minus any Bonuses or Deductions)
Check your Permanent Items chart. Add any Yearly Bonuses to your scores now.
You have now been taxed by the Duke of Pettyham. Subtract one-half of your *Supplies* score.

● If you are under the Earl of Cheshire's rule, he will also expect your tax payment. To pay the tax, subtract one-half of your remaining *Supplies* score or 100, whichever is greater.

● If you are under the Earl of Cheshire's rule and you did not build a water mill last year, subtract an additional one-half from your remaining *Supplies* score to pay the Earl's penalty tax.

● If you want to rebel against the Earl and the Duke, you may choose Actions and Projects to increase your *Defense* score this year.

Step 2: Random Events

Use the Random Events chart on page 96.

Step 3: Goals

Year Six Goal: *Supplies* must reach at least 1,500 before you continue to Step 4.
Choose your Actions and Projects now.
If you are unable to reach a *Supplies* score of 1,500, turn to page 71.

Step 4: Year Six Completion and Bonuses

Bonus For every *Supplies* point you managed to gain above your Goal, give yourself +1 *Effort* point. (For example, a *Supplies* score of 1,725 adds 225 *Effort*.) Add this Bonus to Step 1 in Year Seven.

YEAR SEVEN

The Charter

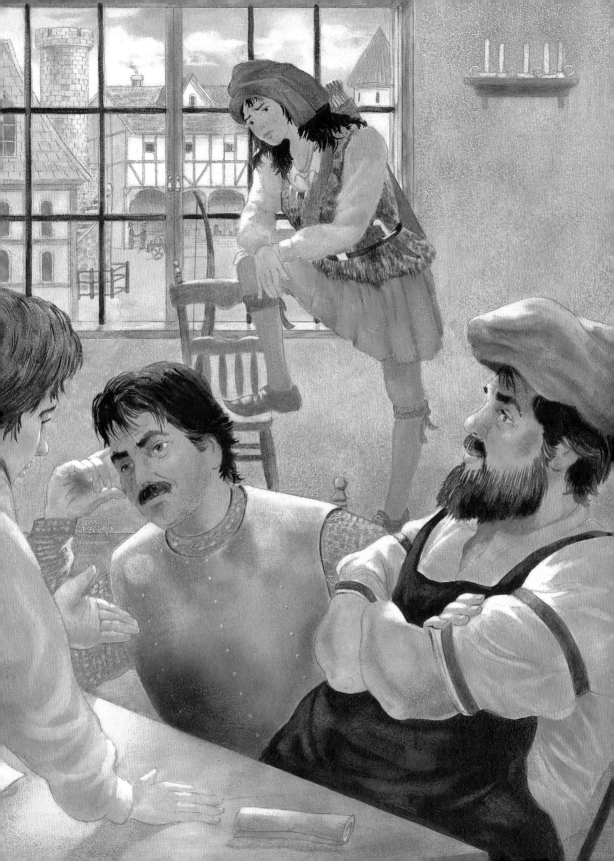

TENSIONS HAVE BEEN HIGH ALL YEAR WITH THE THREAT OF MORE battles, but New Haven, through luck and hard work, has managed to survive. In a moment of desperation, an appeal was sent to the king of England. Little hope was given to the plan, but now, months later, upon the edge of New Haven's lands, a messenger has just galloped away, leaving a parchment in your hands. Your heart quickens as you read …

"What does the Duke want now?" Josephine asks quietly beside you, her catlike eyes narrowing at the path stretching through the wood. She holds her longbow loosely, but you know it can swing into lethal action faster than you can blink. "Or is it the Earl this time with some demand? I have trouble telling their messengers apart."

"Our situation is changing, my friend," you tell her.

"What? Don't tell me that the King himself is coming to our aid?" There is a note of real interest behind her mocking tone.

A Town Charter

The term *town* had a very specific legal meaning in medieval England; that is, a town could not exist without permission and a legal charter. Townspeople differed from peasants and serfs in that charters gave them special privileges and a high degree of freedom to do as they pleased. As long as the townspeople paid their dues, in the form of finished goods, their landlords left them alone. Landlords were usually noblemen who had a great desire for finished fine goods and clothing, and so they encouraged their town residents to hone the skills necessary to supply the noble households with these products. These skills and crafts became the leverage that eventually gave more power and wealth to the workers and merchants than the nobility itself held.

You shake your head. "No. But something nearly as good. Maybe better. We must hurry to the council meeting with this."

Josephine's face is alight with curiosity as the two of you make your way briskly through New Haven. You pass industrious workers at Deborah's tannery, where fresh leathers dry on the line while others are spread out for cutting into the shapes needed for new boots and clothes. Farther up the path, you pass Marcus's woodworks. His two apprentices are tapping barrels together, while another worker is shaving the bark from a newly felled tree. New Haven has been industrious these past two years, making all manner of wares for the Earl.

You and Josephine hurry past all of this. Upon reaching the hall where you have called a meeting of your advisers, you find the discussion already in full swing.

"We are caught between the Duke and the Earl," Marcus bellows. "Each wants us to pay tax, and it doesn't matter which we agree to—the other will see it as fair reason to attack us!"

"But shouldn't paying tax to a lord mean he will offer us protection against others?" Deborah asks.

"That's what they promise," Sir Greggor rumbles. "But more often than not a lord doesn't want to go to the expense and trouble of making war against another powerful noble over a little town like ours. No, he'd rather let the other lord burn us down, and then maybe burn one of *his* towns in retaliation. After all, our lord can still tax us once we've taken the trouble to rebuild." Greggor glowers at the others around the table. "Make no mistake—that's our only value to him."

"That may no longer be true," you say loudly, walking into the middle of the debate. Everybody grows quiet when they see you. "I have received word from the Duke," you continue. "It seems that he and the Earl have learned of our petition to the King for a royal town charter. Duke and Earl have spoken and are offering to cut their tax demands each by half, and that we share it equally with them both … if we agree to drop our petition to the King."

"Can it be?" Albos asks, his face a picture of surprise. "Threat of the King is enough to knock reason into those two thick skulls?"

You explain. "The landlords are afraid of such ideas. They know that the King is very progressive. He is granting many town charters. And when a town is chartered, the town taxes travel directly to the royal treasury in London, and the local lords see not a farthing. The Duke and the Earl are afraid of losing us altogether."

The stunned silence grows cautiously bright.

"No more threat of war?" Mirriam asks. "Is it wise to believe that? They have shown no mercy before now."

"The lords are still very dangerous," you agree quickly. "But we are seeing a change in their attitude. They realize that we are becoming important to their well-being."

Medieval Money

During the medieval period much commerce was done simply by trading goods, but some money did change hands—although it was always metal coins, never paper money. Coins were made from either gold or silver, and the value of each coin was directly linked to the type of metal and how much was used to make the coin.

Clipping Coins

A common and illegal practice was clipping or shaving precious metal from the edges of coins. To combat this problem, King Henry III introduced the *long cross penny*. The cross printed on one side and going right to the edge of the coin made it easy to see if the coin had been clipped.

"Indeed," Deborah Cobbler says, "the Earl himself sent a man this very week, asking that I make a pair of boots for the Earl's son. A full third of my work is for the two lords and their people. And I know Marcus has been doing some carpentry for the Duke ..."

Marcus nods at this dourly. "Aye. My pride is not altogether happy about it, but it is honest work and it keeps my apprentices fed."

"Yes," agrees Albos. "Both the Earl and the Duke have requested my services. This is the first season that I have made horseshoes for both sides."

Everybody considers these promising developments.

"If we are clever about it," you say, "we can make both the Earl and the Duke see the value of keeping New Haven healthy. I believe that neither man wishes to fight forever. Armies are expensive."

Coins of the Realm

In medieval England, the words *pound* and *shilling* were used to describe how much coins were worth, but there were no actual coins with those names. The most valuable coin was called a *noble*. It was made from approximately 8 grams of gold and was worth 20 shillings, or one pound. A shilling was worth 12 pennies, or *pence*. There were several other coins, such as the *half noble*, the *quarter noble*, and the *groat*, which was worth 4 pence. A *half penny* really meant half a penny, and a *farthing* was literally one-fourth of a penny! People would cut pennies into halves and quarters to use when trading for items of very low value.

By the end of the meeting, your advisers understand that New Haven has a tricky path to follow. It must maintain some military defense, but it must not seem so powerful that it threatens the lords and provokes attack. In the meantime, the people must produce enough to keep the town healthy and thriving.

As the meeting adjourns and the various experts, your friends, leave, still discussing the new turn of events, Mirriam Wise wobbles up beside you to pat your arm.

"You've done a good job, dear," she says, her bright eyes sparking at you. "You've led us on quite the adventure these last seven years, from ruin to all these new hopes. I've delivered more babies than I can count, and it's only rarely that I know which ones are marked for something special. But I remember you!" She grins at you without many teeth to show for it. "I remember you."

You laugh in return, and the two of you walk into the morning sunlight arm in arm.

Year Seven Instructions

Learning of New Haven's appeal to King Edward III for a town charter, the Duke and Earl become fearful of alienating your people through taxes or battle. Will the King grant New Haven a town charter? Will you agree to pay taxes to the lords and end the fighting? Important decisions will soon need to be made. But that is another story …

Step 1: Year Beginning Scores

Effort: 1,500 (plus or minus any Bonuses or Deductions)
Supplies: –1,000. Also calculate one-half of your Defense and subtract that number from Supplies.
Check your Permanent Items chart. Add any Yearly Bonuses to your scores now.
If you made friends with the tinkers in the past, then they now agree to live in New Haven permanently, doubling its population. Give yourself an extra 1,500 *Effort* points to work with this year.

Step 2: Random Events

Use the Random Events chart on page 96.

Step 3: Goals

Year Seven Goal: *Supplies* must reach at least 2,000 before you continue to Step 4.
Choose your Actions and Projects now.
If you are unable to reach a *Supplies* score of 1,500, turn to page 71.

Step 4: Year Seven Completion and Bonuses

Congratulations! Your people have survived a most difficult time in their lives and they have you to thank for it. The rest of New Haven's story is up to you. If you'd like to see how New Haven develops in years to come, repeat Steps 1 to 3 above as often as you wish.

Epilogue

OVER THE NEXT HUNDRED YEARS, THE MANY VILLAGES, TOWNS, and cities scattered throughout England struggled beneath the yoke of punishing weather, violent seas, disease, and starvation. By the 1500s, the weather had warmed; color and light once more filled the world. The people of Europe breathed a collective sigh of relief that carried them triumphantly into the bright days of the Renaissance.

New Haven, though a fictional town, depicts one way in which a people might have worked together to survive hardship through cooperation, the use of knowledge, and respect for life.

Failure

New Haven does not survive! Life in 14th-century England was difficult, and the many challenges communities faced were often enough to bring them to a bitter end despite their best efforts. Those who followed you into the Border Marches in hopes of finding new lives are scattered or gone. Some find places for themselves in other regions, while others, less lucky, are lost to hunger, war, and the elements.

Try again. Using your resources carefully and making wise decisions can help overcome bad luck and ensure that your people grow strong and New Haven grows prosperous.

Good luck!

FURTHER READING

This book tells a fictional story about some of the real challenges faced by townspeople in the Middle Ages, but there is a lot more to tell! To find out how the people of a growing town lived, worked, traded, and traveled, try Elliot Lynne's *Medieval Towns, Trade, and Travel* (Crabtree Books, 2004); *Archers, Alchemists, and 98 Other Medieval Jobs You Might Have Loved or Loathed* by Priscilla Galloway with illustrations by Martha Newbigging (Annick Press, 2003); *How Would You Survive in the Middle Ages?* by Fiona MacDonald and David Salariya, illustrated by Mark Peppe (Franklin Watts, 1995); and *Medieval Life* by Andrew Langley (Dorling Kindersley, 2004). Also for more information about the medieval world, visit these websites: www.historyforkids.org/ and www.bbc.co.uk/history/british/middle_ages/.

Sir Greggor Knight
Siege Engineer

SLING

"A simple weapon, this, but in the hands of a practiced soldier it can kill an enemy at a distance."

Effort . . . . . . –100
Supplies . . . –25
Defense . . . . +25

Simple but Deadly

A sling was made of a baton 61 centimeters (2 feet) long, a hanging leather pouch, and a nail hook on one end of the baton to hold the pouch closed. The soldier would lunge forward a few steps and swing the baton so that the pouch unhooked at the critical moment, sending its missile down the field of battle at high speed.

LATRINES

"Oh yes. Quite necessary. In dealing with armies, I've had to learn well how to solve *this* particular problem. Until our village is better established, this field solution will make life more bearable."

[note] You may make latrines once per year during Years One to Three, but not after Year Three.

Effort . . . . . . –25
Supplies . . . +75

Private? No

Military latrines were sometimes made by digging a slit trench in the earth 61 to 91 centimeters (2 to 3 feet) deep, with posts planted at each end. A shin-high beam was set across the tops of the posts to form a simple bench. Soldiers sat and hung their rear ends over this. Trenches were later filled in with earth.

BLACK POWDER

"I've had the chance to use this stuff before. You mix it with oil and wrap a slurry of it about the end of an arrow, and then you've got a blazing missile that won't go out even in water! Good for burning down whole settlements with their thatch rooftops or for burning canvas-covered baggage supply trains. You can't procure enough of the stuff to use it often, but a shot or two is sometimes all you need to turn the tide of battle."

Supplies . . .–400

Fire, Smoke, and Fury

Made from saltpeter, imported from China, and also called Chinese Snow, black powder was rare and expensive in medieval Europe. It was used in both hand cannons and incendiary weapons.

HAND CANNON

"What a weapon! Loud as thunder, with a great dragon's cough of smoke. Fire one of those in battle, and you'll strike fear and astonishment into a whole attacking troop and gain the advantage by that means alone. A danger if it misfires, and costly to build, but set off at the right moment it might be quite effective."

Prerequisites:
• blacksmithy (see page 88)
• black powder (see above)

Supplies . . .–450
Defense . . . .To score for Defense,
          roll a die.
            –300 (if you roll 1)
            +250 (if you roll 2 or 3)
            +500 (if you roll 4 or 5)
            +750 (if you roll 6)

The Early Firearm

The hand cannon was a new invention, first appearing around the 1380s, and one of the first military applications of black powder. A short bronze pipe about 30 centimeters (1 foot) long was lashed to a pole called a *tiller* and held like a staff. When it was lit and aimed (with both hands holding on very firmly), the hand cannon could shoot through armor and easily knock a soldier from a warhorse.

➤ WATCHTOWER

"A very good idea and not so hard to build. We'll see the enemy much sooner and be able to raise an alarm. That way, no ugly surprises!"

Prerequisite:
• barrels (see page 80)

Effort . . . . . .–100
Supplies . . .–50
Defense . . . .+100

[note] You may only have two watchtowers.

SMALL, ROPE-PULLED CATAPULTS AND TREBUCHETS

"With a big lever arm fixed on a triangular frame, a sling, ammunition, ropes, and a gang of 10 or so people to work it, this is a wonder fixed to the top of a wall. Put it on a swivel and you can aim it nicely!"

Prerequisite:
• *cord and rope (see page 92)*

Effort . . . . . . –400
Supplies . . . –200
Defense . . . . +400

Launching with Precision

Small catapults were highly accurate and could be reloaded to fire every 15 seconds. A 2.25 kilogram (5 pound) missile could be launched to a target area 3 square meters (32 square feet) from as far away as 165 meters (180 yards). Mounted cavalry needed about 30 seconds to cover that distance; thus a few small catapults could make their path treacherous.

Stones from the Sky

The large trebuchet could be very accurate if the missiles were carefully weighed. With repeated strikes, the toughest walls could be reduced to rubble. The counterweight that powered this device could weigh several tons, and the missiles weighed 91 to 136 kilograms (200 to 300 pounds).

LARGE, WEIGHT-PULLED CATAPULTS AND TREBUCHETS

"This is a dandy of a war engine against a castle, and a devastating weapon."

Prerequisites:
• *lumber (see page 80)*
• *cord and rope (see page 92)*

Effort . . . . . . –400
Supplies . . . –400
Defense . . . . +500

Muscles and Mechanics

Ancient catapults were spring-powered by twisting rope. By the 1400s, this approach had given way to human-powered and weight-pulled war machines.

GABIONS

"These walls are an excellent strategic tool on the battlefield—and easy to transport; just dump out the rocks!"

Effort . . . . . . –250
Supplies . . .–50
Defense . . . .+100 (or +200 if you have battle arrows; see page 90)

Sticks and Stones Protect the Bones

A gabion is a barrier made from willow branches woven with *wattle and daub* (mud mixed with wool, leaves, and twigs) into hollow cylinders. These are then filled with earth and rocks, like a big barrel. Two or three of these could be put into place to form a temporary cover from enemy arrows and even cannonballs.

➤ PALISADE

"Those who would attack us will often come on horse-back. Because we might only muster foot soldiers, a palisade with a few archers will give us an advantage against a force of mounted nobles."

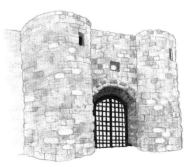

Prerequisites:
• *lumber (see page 80)*
• *carts and wagons (see page 81)*

Effort . . . . . . –400
Supplies . . .–400
Defense . . . .+400 (or +500 if you have battle arrows; see page 90)

The Fort

A palisade was a simple but effective wall made from sharpened logs stood on end, planted in trenches, and lashed together. With earth piled up at the base on the defender's side, palisades were a solid and reasonably quick way to circle a fort or settlement. Palisades were usually built on high ground—sometimes a hill built from rocks and earth to encircle the settlement—giving the defending soldiers the advantage, the "high ground."

➤ STONE BARBICAN WITH IRON GATES

"We would build a half-round tower of stone to fortify the entranceway to New Haven. Most attacks focus on the way in, so we'd be best to make it as strong as possible!"

Prerequisites:
• *blacksmithy (see page 88)*
• *carts and wagons (see page 81)*

[note] You may build the stone barbican only once.

Effort . . . . . . –2000
Supplies . . .–1500
Defense . . . .+2000 (or +5000 if you have battle arrows; see page 90)

Experts' Catalog

Mirriam Wise
Homestead Elder

HEALING HERBS

"Fennel, parsley, onions, leeks, sage, borage, and lovage. Some things I grow can help to cure many ailments."

[note] You may grow herbs twice a year if you wish.

Effort . . . . . . −200 (or −100 if you have any farming tools, either wooden or metal; see pages 81 and 89)
Supplies. . . . +300

FOOD GATHERING AND PRESERVING

"Berries, nuts, fruit, greens, and all edible roots, my dear. That includes mushrooms too—but only the ones I tell you are safe to pick!"

Effort . . . . . −25
Supplies . . .+25

Medieval Drugs

St. John's wort, feverfew, spikenard, hemlock, opium, and henbane were some of the drugs available. These were administered as hot drinks and they were not really considered different from regular foods. Medicine was not a well-understood concept in medieval Europe. For example, lettuce was believed to help nursing mothers produce milk because its sap was milky in color.

VEGETABLE GARDEN

"Carrots, beets, and other root vegetables for the stew pot to make it taste aright. All of this and more we can grow right in our yards. A good garden will provide a great wealth of food to keep us strong and whole."

[note] You may grow a vegetable garden twice a year if you wish.

Effort . . . . . . −200 (or −100 if you have any farming tools, either wooden or metal; see pages 81 and 89)
Supplies. . . . +250

CROP HARVEST

"Grain is needed for bread and for feeding livestock. We will need to grow oats, rye, barley, and more."

Prerequisite:
• *plow or farming tools (see page 89 for metal farming tools and plow, page 81 for wooden farming tools)*

Effort . . . . . . −250 (if you have wooden farming tools)
−200 (if you have metal farming tools)
−150 (if you have a plow)
−100 (if you have an ox and a plow; for ox, see page 86)
Supplies. . . . +400

SOAP

"It is my belief that disease comes in part from dirt and stink!"

Prerequisite:
• *animal snare or large game (if successful) or small game or small livestock (see pages 85, 86, and 87)*

[note] You may make soap up to three times a year.

Effort . . . . . . −25
Supplies. . . . +75

Old Soap
Soap was made from ashes, called *pot-ash*, and animal fats mixed together in vats and then poured into molds.

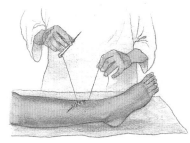

SURGERY

"I can set broken bones better than if naught is done at all, and I can sew up wounds. It is a tricky thing, mind. More difficult procedures I will perform when I must, but I cannot promise success."

[note] You may perform surgery once per year.

Effort . . . . . −50
Supplies . . .To score for Supplies, roll a die.
−250 (if you roll 1–3)
+150 (if you roll 4–6)
+250 (if you roll 4–6 and made soap this year; see above)

Dangerous Medicine
Surgery was dangerous and painful in medieval Europe. *Trepanning* (drilling holes in the skull to relieve pressure) was used to combat recurring headaches. Removing bladder stones was often more deadly than the condition.

CLOTH MAKING

"If we want to be warm, we need clothes to wear and cloth for clothes."

Prerequisites:
• *small livestock (see page 86) or crop harvest (see page 77)*
• *spinning whorl (see page 92)*

Effort . . . . . .–150
Supplies . . .+300

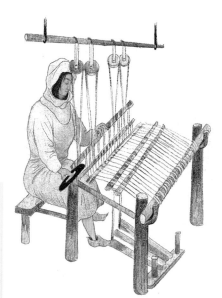

A Different Cloth

Two main fibers made medieval fabric: sheep's wool and linen. Wool was shorn from sheep, cleaned, combed, and woven. The rough wool fabric was then softened in a combination of aged urine and a type of clay, then pounded. If this was done for long enough, it turned the fabric into a soft felt, which held off the rain and cold. Linen is made from flax leaves—the same plant used in making ropes. The leaves were softened by soaking, pounded open, and stripped of their fibers with a comb; then the fiber was spun into thread, which was woven into cloth.

BEER BREWING

"Beer is a wonder! It won't make us sick like the changeable water from the river."

Prerequisites:
• *crop harvest (see page 77)*
• *barrels (see page 80)*

Effort . . . . .–300
Supplies . . .+400

Clean and Bitter

In the 14th century, everybody from the smallest child to the oldest senior drank beer! People's bodies were adapted to tolerate the low alcohol content (about 3 percent), which was enough to kill bacteria in what was commonly dirty water. Beer was a safe way to get water into the diet.

The Making of Beer

Beer in the 14th century was sweet-tasting, made from barley. The barley was soaked until it began to sprout, releasing its sugar. Then it was roasted and mashed in a large bath of water. Yeast from the last batch of beer was added, which fermented the mixture. After several days of brewing, the beer was filtered for drinking. Beer would last about two weeks in storage.

HAND-GRINDING GRAIN

"Tsk . . . this is one of those tiresome necessities of life. We simply cannot do without flour to make our bread, so somebody must be at the quern all day, every day, turning the stone."

Prerequisite:
- *crop harvest (see page 77)*

Effort . . . . . . –50

Rancid Flour
In medieval times, grains could be stored for a long time, but flour could not be kept more than a couple of weeks before the insects, rats, and mold did their work. Flour had to be freshly ground on a regular basis—and you could tell a hard-working woman of the time by looking at the muscles on her arms.

The Daily Grind
Every household in the 14th century had a grindstone—usually a combination of two: a flat, round stone called a *quern* and one on top turned by a handle. Grains were poured between the stones and ground into flour.

A Baker's Pinch
Because many families would share one bake oven, often one person would work the oven and the others would bring their dough to the baker. The baker would take a pinch from each ball of dough in order to make one extra. The extra was considered fair payment to the baker for running the communal oven.

BREAD MAKING

"Bread is one of the most important foods we have. Every family will want to make bread."

Prerequisites:
- *crop harvest (see page 77)*
- *grain grinding (from this year)—by hand or by either a horizontal water mill or a vertical water mill (see page 83)*
- *bake oven (see page 81)*

Effort . . . . . –50 for every 400 Supplies gained
Supplies . . .+400 (if you hand-grind grain using a quern)
+800 (if you have a horizontal water mill)
+1600 (if you have a vertical water mill)

Experts' Catalog

Marcus Wainwright
Master Carpenter

LUMBER

"We'll be needing cut wood, sure enough, or I'll not be able to ply my trade. Give me a team and we'll get started at once. We'll turn that wood into planks and beams, you'll see!"

Prerequisite:
• *carpentry tools (see page 88)*

Effort . . . . . .–200 (per item)

No Bark, No Rot

Rot happens in the bark. *Dressing down* a log, or removing the bark, was an important job. After dressing down, a log was called a *perline*.

Preparing the Wood

Construction-grade lumber was split along the grain using axes and wedges. Sawing was only done across the grain. Planks were roughly shaped with a special ax called an *adze*. There was no sandpaper in the 14th century, so planes and flat pumice stones made from sandstone were used to finish wood.

➤ BARRELS

"Ah, yes. We'll be needing many of these, large and small, for everything from cups to vats. I'll teach some of the young men the cooper's craft."

Prerequisite:
• *lumber (see above)*

Effort . . . . .–125
Supplies . . .+50 every year for every set of barrels made

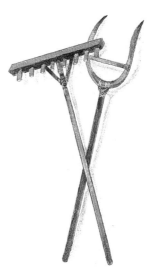

➤ WOODEN FARMING TOOLS

"If we are to sow and reap the earth, we will need all manner of tools. Rakes and hoes, flails and harrows, and the mulboard plow—although many of these items will work much better with the help of Master Albos and his blacksmithy …"

Prerequisite:
• *lumber (see page 80)*

Effort . . . . . .−100

➤ CARTS AND WAGONS

"Excellent, useful devices to be certain—we'll be needing several of these to make all manner of heavy work lighter."

Prerequisites:
• *lumber (see page 80)*
• *carpentry tools (see page 88)*

Effort . . . . . .−200
Supplies . . .+300

Two Wheels

Over 80 percent of carts in medieval Europe had only two wheels. Effective four-wheel vehicles required gear technology that had not been developed. Two-wheel carts limited hauling size, but were quite useful.

➤ BAKE OVEN

"A long day's work deserves a good bit of bread at both ends of it. Oven building is a fine craft, to be sure. Lucky thing I like my bread well enough to learn it!"

Effort . . . . . .−200

Home and Hearth

Bake ovens were big stone structures that were domed inside. Fires were built inside to heat the stone and then scraped out. Bread dough was put in on slats. Each oven was shared by many families; a community of 50 families might have two or three ovens.

➤ FRAME HOUSE

"Oh, yes. I can build a house just as fine as you like—two floors if you like, three even, with stairs and good walls and a roof to keep the rain off ye."

Prerequisites:
- *lumber (see page 80)*
- *carpentry tools (see page 88)*

[note] You may only build two houses each year.

Effort . . . . . . –350
Supplies . . .+200 every year per house

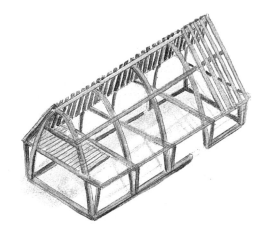

Medieval Houses

Frame houses had timber beams and walls of *wattle and daub* (mud mixed with wool, leaves, and twigs). These sturdy dwellings used a timber truss with a straw roof—and they could be very cold in the winter.

➤ SMOKEHOUSE

"Ah, to have meat all year, we must smoke it. I'll build us our smokehouse."

Prerequisite:
- *lumber (see page 80)*

[note] You may have only one smokehouse.

Effort . . . . . . –250
Supplies . . .+150

Curing Meat

A smokehouse was a low building, often covered with sod, with a slow fire kept burning inside for curing meat and fish. Once smoked, meats could be kept at room temperature for longer periods of time without going bad.

Vermin!

Rats were a huge drain on the local economy, eating grain and flour in storage and anything else they could reach. Cats were very useful for helping to keep the rat population down.

➤ COMMON BARN

"Our village will need two or three barns for all our livestock and storage."

Prerequisite:
• *lumber (see page 80)*

[note] You may have no more than three barns.

Effort . . . . . . –325
Supplies . . .+200 every year per barn

Keeping Warm and Dry
Barns were made from wood, sometimes with stone walls. Posts were set into the ground to hold up a roof of wood planks covered with cedar or pine shingles.

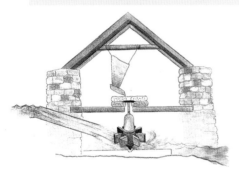

➤ HORIZONTAL WATER MILL

"This is a clever device. It uses a smaller stone and is far less difficult to make than the vertical water mill, but it is no good in the winter."

Prerequisites:
• *millwright (see Year Five)*
• *lumber (see page 80)*
• *carts and wagons (see page 81)*

[note] You may only build a mill during or after Year Five.

Effort . . . . . . –500

➤ VERTICAL WATER MILL

"Now this is the pinnacle of the craft! A bit beyond my abilities, I'm afraid, but with the right help I can do my part in constructing one of these beasts!"

Prerequisites:
• *millwright (see Year Five)*
• *lumber (see page 80)*
• *carts and wagons (see page 81)*

[note] You may only build a mill during or after Year Five.

Effort . . . . . . –1000

Stone from Cologne
All grindstones for water mills in 14th-century England came from the Rhine Valley, near Cologne, and were called *cullen stones*. The stones were 122 to 168 centimeters (4 to 5.5 feet) in diameter and were used as ship ballast during transport. Millwrights cut and *dressed* these stones, shaving a special pattern into them so that the milling process would work. They did this work on the site of the new mill.

Josephine Fletcher
Archer, Hunter, Trapper

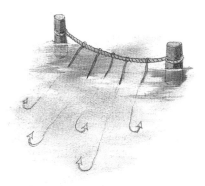

FISHING LINE AND HOOK

"We can fish our little river using a fan of fishing lines made from thin cord and many hooks—a fine way to catch a goodly number of fish. We already have shaped bone and wire for our hooks."

Prerequisite:
• *cord and rope (see page 92)*

Effort . . . . . . –100
Supplies . . . .+150 (or +175 if you have a smokehouse; see page 82)

River Fish
Salmon, whiteling, and grayfish were common in English rivers during the 14th century and provided a good source of food.

FISHING NET
"This is a nice, easy way to catch many fish if we trawl. The only trouble is keeping the nets in repair …"

Prerequisite:
• *cord and rope (see page 92)*

Effort . . . . . . –200
Supplies . . .+400 (or +500 if you have a
smokehouse; see page 82)

Netting Dinner
Very strong nets were made using thick linen cord tied in a repeating pattern. Net makers used a netting frame and a *fid*, a rod made from ivory, to tie the nets.

ANIMAL SNARE OR NET

"Good for catching hares and badgers and such. I'll whip up a few of these so's we've got a steady supply of little beasts to put in the dinner pot."

[note] You may do this twice per year.

Effort . . . . . . –75
Supplies . . .To score for Supplies, roll a die.
+0 (if you roll 1 or 2)
+100 (if you roll 3 or 4)
+200 (if you roll 5 or 6)

Snap!
Snares were made from twine and sticks and flexible trees. Hunters set traps in the morning and checked them the following day.

BOW AND ARROW

"The bow is a thing of grace and speed. The skilled shooter can both feed her family and fend away the braggarts who would disturb their peace."

Prerequisite:
• *cord and rope (see page 92)*

Effort . . . . . . –200
Defense . . . .+200 (or +400 if you have a quiver; see page 94)

Arming the Archer
Hunting bows were made with wood from the yew tree, specially prepared to be flexible, and with strong cord. Shafts had to be straight; they were carefully split and carved, then the skilled *fletcher* would affix the metal head and tail feathers.

The Hunt
Deer and wild boar were the only big game hunted in 14th-century England. The beasts were pursued with hounds, cornered, and then killed with bows, crossbows, and spears.

➤ SMALL LIVESTOCK

"A few sheep will serve us well for their wool and meat, goats for their milk, and ducks and hens for eggs. Pigs breed quickly and they make for good eating."

Prerequisite:
• *crop harvest (see page 77)*

Effort . . . . . . –200 (or –100 if you have dogs and a dog kennel; see page 87)
Supplies . . . +200 (every year for each investment in small livestock) (or +225 if you have a smokehouse; see page 82)

➤ OX

"A single ox is a great boon! Oxen pull the plows and carts, and when their work life is done, they promise many soups and stews. I know the mind of such animals, and I will teach our people in their care."

Prerequisites:
• *crop harvest (see page 77)*
• *common barn (see page 83)*

Effort . . . . . . –200
Supplies . . . +250 (every year for each ox) (or +275 if you have a smokehouse; see page 82)

➤ RIDING HORSE

"A horse is a fine creature, elegant and wise, and a great benefit for long journeys or in matters of war. But they are rather expensive to feed …"

Prerequisites:
• *crop harvest (see page 77)*
• *common barn (see page 83)*

Effort . . . . . . –300
Supplies . . . +200
Defense . . . . +100 (or +500 if you have a harness and saddle for this horse; see page 95)

SMALL GAME

"Give me some nets and a few dogs, and we can catch hares, conies, and birds by the bunch."

Prerequisite:
• *cord and rope (see page 92)*

Effort . . . . . .–150 (or –100 if you have dogs and a dog kennel; see below)
Supplies . . .+300 (or +375 if you have a smoke-house; see page 82)

Different Long Ears
Conies are rabbits. As barnyard animals, they were first raised in Normandy. Hares, which are larger and stronger, ran wild throughout England.

Feathers and Fur
With dogs (to bark and chase the small game) and beaters (helpers with sticks, to disturb the bushes), small game animals were stampeded into nets. Birds were also caught in nets strung between trees and poles, and their feathers were used for pillows and brooms. In contrast, aristocrats hunted with falcons.

LARGE GAME

"A single deer or boar can provide a great deal of meat to feed many people, as well as leather for clothing and gut for cord."

Prerequisite:
• *bow and arrow (see page 85)*

[note] You may hunt large game three times per year.

Effort . . . . . .–200 (or –100 if you have dogs and a dog kennel; see below)
Supplies . . .To score for Supplies, roll a die.
+0 (if you roll 1)
+400 (if you roll 2–4, or +500 if you have a smokehouse; see page 82)
+500 (if you roll 5 or 6, or +625 if you have a smokehouse; see page 82)

➤ DOGS AND DOG KENNEL

"Hunting hounds are wonderful creatures—likable and useful. They earn their keep well enough, and they'll rest their heads in our laps."

Effort . . . . . .–200
Supplies . . .–200

Experts' Catalog

Albos Black
Blacksmith

➤ BLACKSMITHY
"This is where I will rebuild my smithy. Luckily, I was able to rescue my tools and my anvil from the ruins of Port Haven. It's a blessing that iron is not so light and ready to be washed out to sea!"

Effort . . . . . . –500

The Medieval Blacksmithy
A 14th-century blacksmithy was outfitted with an anvil, a selection of hammers and tongs, a forge, a supply of charcoal fuel, and an assistant to work the bellows. Thus equipped, a blacksmith could produce all manner of metal items, including nails, hinges, horseshoes, tools, knives, swords, and various other weapons.

SMALL HARDWARE
"There's no end to all the bits and bobs a growing village needs: nails, hooks, hinges, clasps, wire, chain links, and any other shape iron might need banging into!"

Prerequisite:
• *blacksmithy (see above)*

Effort . . . . . . –25
Supplies . . . +25

Bog Iron
The silts in the wet, spongy ground of bogs naturally collect iron oxide. When these silts are fossilized, the resulting shale rock is rich in the mineral. In the Middle Ages, blacksmiths would smelt the shale with charcoal (to melt out the iron) and limestone (to prevent oxidation). The raw metal stock, called *bog iron*, was made into flat bars about 61 centimeters (2 feet) long. Bog iron was low-grade by modern standards but useful in the Middle Ages and widely traded.

➤ CARPENTRY TOOLS
"Master Marcus will have need of these items, and that's no lie. Axes and saws, planes and chisels, gouges and augers and all. You cannot do much with wood without iron."

Prerequisite:
• *blacksmithy (see above)*

Effort . . . . . . –100

➤ METAL FARMING TOOLS

"I can make scythes and sickles, as well as the joints and fittings that will make all of Marcus's farm tools work much better."

Prerequisites:
• *blacksmithy (see page 88)*
• *wooden farming tools (see page 81)*

Effort . . . . . .–100

➤ PLOW

"I can put together a plow that will actually work, my friend! Metal armor fastened to the cutting edge of the plow is the key."

Prerequisites:
• *blacksmithy (see page 88)*
• *wooden farming tools (see page 81)*

Effort . . . . . .–200

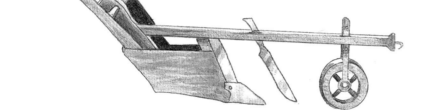

KNIVES

"I can make a reasonable-enough knife, if the quality of the iron is any good. After I've made one, it will serve its holder well if it is kept clean, sharp, and oiled."

Prerequisite:
• *blacksmithy (see page 88)*

Effort . . . . . .–100
Supplies . . .+100
Defense . . . .+50

A Knife in Every Belt
In England during the medieval period, every boy over 12 years old carried a knife, from the lowliest shepherd to the mightiest prince. Blades were often crude and measured 13 to 15 centimeters (5 to 6 inches) in length.

SWORDS

"A sword? Well, yes, I do know how, but it's the getting of the good iron that is the challenge, and then the process is not an easy one."

Prerequisite:
• *blacksmithy (see page 88)*

```
Effort . . . . . . –1000
Supplies  . . .–500
Defense . . . .+1000
```

A Mark of Wealth

Swords were more difficult to make than knives because the quality of the iron had to be higher in order to make blades both flexible enough not to snap and hard enough to hold an edge. In the 14th century, swords were affordable to the noble class but out of reach to the peasant farmer: one sword would cost a peasant farmer the equivalent of four months' pay.

BATTLE ARROWS

"This is a different breed of arrowhead. We must have many of these, so I'll make them in my spare time and keep them until we need them—though I hope we never will!"

Prerequisites:
• *blacksmithy (see page 88)*
• *bow and arrow (see page 85)*

```
Effort . . . . . . –200
Supplies  . . .–200
Defense . . . .+300 (or +600 if you also purchase
                black powder; see page 73)
```

Arrows—Long and Sleek

Hunting arrowheads were longer and sleeker, designed for soft targets. These arrowheads were about the same length as battle arrowheads, but their knife edges flared to about half the width.

Arrows—Wide and Many

Battle arrowheads were deadly in design: from tip to socket they were about 8 to 10 centimeters (3 to 4 inches) long, with flaring knife-edge blades 5 centimeters (2 inches) wide. Blacksmiths mass-produced them, and it was common for a village to store as many as 2000 battle arrowheads. The arrowheads were stored separately from the shafts, and the arrows were assembled later, closer to when they were needed.

SHIELDS

"When the enemy is hurling all its might against us, it is good to have something to take cover behind."

Prerequisite:
• *blacksmithy (see page 88)*

Effort . . . . . .–200
Supplies . . .–200
Defense . . . .+300

Shields as Weapons

Shields could be used for defense against swords and small projectiles *and* as weapons themselves. The better ones often had sharpened edges designed for this purpose.

PLATE ARMOR

"Metal to cover one's trunk, head, and limbs only makes sense in combat on the field. Without it, our troops will be cut down quickly."

Prerequisite:
• *blacksmithy (see page 88)*

Effort . . . . . .–400
Supplies . . .–500
Defense . . . .+500

The End of the Chain (Mail)

In the 14th century, plate armor was common. Chain mail took much more effort to fabricate and was seen far less often—mainly used along with plate armor. One piece of chain mail was the *aventail*, which hung from a helmet to protect the neck.

Deborah Cobbler
Shoemaker, leather
and cord worker

➤ SPINNING WHORL

"This is the tool I use to make threads and strings and smallish cords. I hang it like so and tie the material to the bottom, and then spin it round and round like a top on a string!"

Effort . . . . . .–100
Supplies . . .+100

CORD AND ROPE

"Cords and ropes are some of the most useful and necessary tools ever invented. You need bows and fishing lines? You want something to tie up, herd, and harness our riding and toiling beasts? You want to build a rabbit snare? You want to build a catapult of any worth? I'll get to work at once."

Prerequisite:
• *spinning whorl (see above)*

Effort . . . . . .–50 (per item)

Flax and Hemp

Flax is the plant used to make linen, and it was also used for early ropes. Hemp is a very strong weed, and from the 14th to the 19th century in Europe, it dominated the rope industry and was used in ship rigging and anywhere else long, strong ropes were needed.

Hide, Hair, and More

Many types of cord and rope were made from animals. Tanned leather cut into long strips was used in single lengths or braided together to make tough rope. Sinews from muscles or intestines stretched, twisted, and dried made strong, thin cord. Animal hair—from horse tail or sheep wool—was woven into long, useful cord. However, long grasses and tough weeds were also used to make excellent rope.

TENT
"Canvas, rope, pegs, and poles. Simple enough, light to pack, and a good-enough way to keep our people dry and warm."

Prerequisite:
• *cord and rope (see page 92)*

[note] You may make tents once per year.

Effort . . . . . . –100
Supplies . . .+250

Simple Shelter
Tents were set up on raised ground to avoid rain runoff. With some straw underfoot, they were both a simple and a comfortable shelter even in harsh weather.

Continental Canvas
At the end of the 14th century, England sent harvested flax to Flanders as thread, where it was made into canvas and bought back. The English exported a lot of wool to continental Europe for similarly finished products.

Cloth Ruled Europe
In 14th-century England and continental Europe, the cloth merchants were among the richest and most powerful citizens. Cloth was in demand all over Europe, and huge baggage trains called *caravans* were used to transport the goods. Because caravans traveled regularly and were well protected, they became a means of transport for many other goods.

Horns Unrolled
Animal horn is bone similar to fingernail, but twice as thick and rolled up. When it is boiled until soft enough, it can be unrolled into sheets, which can then be used to make cups, scoops, spoons, and even windows. Horn was also used for finger and arm guards for combat archers and for simple body armor.

HORN
"A most interesting material. Bring me goat horns and I'll give you nice, glossy waterproof sheets to make all manner of useful things."

Prerequisite:
• *small livestock (see page 86)*

[note] You may craft horn up to three times per year.

Effort . . . . . . –25
Supplies . . .+75

➤ TANNERY

"Oh, this is quite the disgusting mess of a job, but ever so necessary. I hope people remember, when they shun the stink, that the fine shoes they walk away wearing are owed to my efforts here."

Effort ......−200

Foul-Smelling Business

To make leather, tanners conditioned animal skins with greasy manure (mostly dog feces, because of the high fat content) and putrefied urine (for the ammonia). They were often up to their elbows in the stuff, and the occupation was considered dirty and low in status. Tanning was always done at the edge of the community and downstream.

BOOTS AND SHOES

"I know I am certainly happier to have my feet covered up in the cold mornings. I'll have my workers making or repairing shoes near every day."

Prerequisites:
- *tannery (see above)*
- *small livestock or small game or large game (see pages 86 and 87)*

Effort ......−100
Supplies ...+150

QUIVER

"A bow without a quiver makes a hunter or a soldier slow in the moments when it counts most!"

Prerequisites:
- *tannery (see above)*
- *small livestock or small game or large game (see pages 86 and 87)*

Effort ......−100

The Quiver

When hunting, an archer would wear a quiver slung over the back to allow for easier hiking through woods and bush. During battle, however, archers wore quivers on their belts. This made it harder to walk or run, but the archer had faster access to the ammunition. An experienced combat archer was able to unleash an arrow about every five seconds.

LEATHER ARMOR

"Sir Greggor has been making his grumbling noises at me. He says he wants me to provide him with hard armor for our soldier men. Ought I to indulge him?"

Prerequisites:
- *tannery (see page 94)*
- *small livestock or small game (see pages 86 and 87)*

Effort . . . . . . –200
Supplies . . .–200
Defense . . . .+400

[note] You may make leather armor twice per year.

> ### Hardened Leather
> To make leather stiff and hard enough to be used as simple plate armor, leather workers would boil the leather.

➤ BOOK AND PARCHMENT

"Knowledge is a powerful thing. When we can record and study what we know, any task can become easier to do better."

Prerequisites:
- *tannery (see page 94)*
- *small livestock or small game (see pages 86 and 87)*

[note] You may make one book per year.

Effort . . . . . .–300

[note] Each year, increase by 10 percent your scores for Effort, Supplies, and Defense for each book you own—to a maximum of 50 percent.

> ### Horseback Battle
> In battle, riders used saddles to help stay on the horse's back while fighting. Otherwise, peasants rode bareback—if they rode at all.

HORSE HARNESS AND SADDLE

"Oh, to battle we are preparing, are we? Well then, these will be a good idea. I imagine falling from horseback on one's rear end is a less than clever tactic when fighting villains!"

Prerequisites:
- *tannery (see page 94)*
- *ox or large game (see pages 86 and 87)*

Effort . . . . . . –200
Supplies . . .–150

> ### Medieval Ink
> Ink was made by mixing pulverized gallbladders (for the tannic acid) with ferrous sulfate and gum. When made properly, the result was an excellent permanent black ink. When the mixtures were not well balanced, the ink became acidic and would eventually burn through parchment. Many old books and scrolls have been lost because of acidic ink.

> ### Paper from Skin
> To make parchment, sheepskin was soaked in lime for 3 to 10 days, then stretched and dried on a frame. Next, the skin was scraped with a circular knife called a *lunellarium*. The skin was re-wetted and pounded with pumice stone and chalk to give it a smooth, white surface suitable for receiving ink.

Random Events

Roll a six-sided die. If you roll …

1. **HARSH WEATHER**—The sun and rains, bad as they have been, were worse this year, making for a poor growing season. Subtract 300 from Supplies.
2. **GOOD WEATHER**—An excellent growing season! Add 200 to Supplies or, if you have barrels, add 400 to Supplies.
3. **BANDITS ATTACK**—If Defense is 500 or greater, subtract 0 from Supplies.
   If Defense is 200–499, subtract 200 from Supplies.
   If Defense is less than 200, subtract 500 from Supplies.
4. **TINKERS!**—If you allowed the tinkers to stay in Year Three, then roll on the Trade and Tinker chart at the right. If not, or if it is Year One or Two, no random events take place; go back to your Year Instructions and follow Step 3.
5. **GOOD HUNTING**—Josephine has a good year! Add 100 to Supplies or, if you have a smokehouse, add 400 to Supplies.
6. **PLAGUE AND SICKNESS**—You can do one of two things:
   a) Confine the sick and their families until they are either healed or dead. Subtract 300 from this year's Effort.*
   b) Do nothing. Roll a die and multiply that number by 100; subtract the total from Effort.*

Trade and Tinker

Roll a six-sided die. If you roll …

1. **TINKERS' TREAT!**—Excellent dealings with the tinkers this year. Add 300 to Supplies.
2. **THEFT!**—The tinkers have stolen from you. Subtract 300 from Supplies.
3. **USEFUL NEWS**—The tinkers inform you about bandit activities in the Border Marches. Add 200 to Defense.
4. **GOOD TRADE**—At no cost, you may have any one item in the Experts' Catalog that is NOT a building or permanent structure, and which has a combined Effort and Supplies cost of 400 or less. Ignore any prerequisites for this item.
5. **HIRED HANDS**—Pay tinkers to assist in village work. You may deduct up to 500 points from Supplies and add them to your Effort score. Do this now.
6. **PLAGUE**—The tinkers bring the plague! You can do one of two things:
   a) Confine the sick and their families until they are either healed or dead. Subtract 300 from this year's Effort.*
   b) Do nothing. Roll a die and multiply that number by 100; subtract the total from Effort.*

*Add back 50 Effort for each set of healing herbs grown last year.

Battle

If your Defense score is . . .	Result	Effect on Score
0–249	New Haven suffers the full brunt of the attack.	• Roll a die and multiply that number by 300. Subtract that total from this year's starting Effort score. • Reduce your Supplies score by half. Reduce it by half again. • Reduce Defense to 0.
250–749	You repel the troops but suffer heavy losses.	• Roll a die and multiply that number by 200. Subtract that total from this year's starting Effort score. • Reduce your Supplies score by half. • Subtract 250 from Defense.
750–1,499	You repel the troops but suffer moderate losses.	• Roll a die and multiply that number by 100. Subtract that total from this year's starting Effort score. • Reduce your Supplies score by one-quarter (half of one-half). • Subtract 250 from Defense.
1,500 or greater	You repel all the troops and suffer only minor losses.	• Subtract 250 from Defense.

If your Supplies score reaches 0, turn to page 71.

DATE DUE